039588

RANCH LIFE IN THE FAR WEST

Reprinted from Century Magazine

RANCH LIFE
IN THE FAR WEST

By *THEODORE ROOSEVELT*

Illustrated by FREDERIC REMINGTON

NORTHLAND PRESS · FLAGSTAFF ARIZONA

PREFACE

Theodore Roosevelt, the colorful twenty-sixth president of the United States, and Frederic Remington, an artist called a "national treasure," became friends and a working team many years before they were internationally known. Although they were an unlikely pair, with very little in common, they found in 1888 that they shared a similar emotion—a passion for the Old West.

From their dissimilar vantage points, these native New Yorkers each displayed more than a mild preoccupation with the West that was in the throes of a rapid demise. In 1883 they were unaware that they lived only a few hundred miles apart in the Great Plains. While Remington was in Kansas trying to make a go of it on a small sheep ranch, Roosevelt was establishing a partnership in the Chimney Butte cattle ranch in Dakota Territory. Located near the Territory's northwest border, the ranch was about eight miles from Medora. The Little Missouri meanders through the area where the Badlands are a constant reminder that man is not always in command. The scorching heat of summer and the long freezing winters are uncompromising. It is as if the elements test man's desire to survive and to flourish from the land. It was here that Roosevelt built his own Elkhorn Ranch, down the river from the one he and his partners shared. The home on the ranch was constructed of logs and was larger than most in the area. From his long veranda, shaded by the musical leaves of the cottonwoods, Roosevelt often relaxed in a rocking chair and read. If he looked up and out over the land he had a breathtaking view of high-rising cliffs which formed a backdrop for a peaceful meadow. When he first arrived in the area, he was well aware that the locals called him the "four-eyed tenderfoot." Their attitude changed, though, when he worked with them hour after hour; during one round-up, he stayed in the saddle forty hours and exhausted five horses. When he sat with the cowboys around the campfire at the end of the work days and traded stories, he felt the friendship they had for a fellow worker.

In 1884, Remington had gone broke in Kansas and moved westward to sketch the rapidly changing environment. Simultaneously in the East, *Century* and *Outing* magazines were issuing Roosevelt's articles about the Old West. By

v

the time Roosevelt put together a series of stories on ranch life and the many kinds of two- and four-legged animals he had known out West, Remington returned to New York with a full portfolio of drawings. Fortunately, it came together with perfect timing in 1888, when *Century* arranged with Roosevelt to publish his series on *Ranch Life in the Far West*. The writer had seen the western illustrations of the almost-unknown Remington and was convinced only he could graphically and accurately convey the realities of ranch life. It probably took very little discussion from Roosevelt to convince the editor of *Century* that Remington was the best man for the job.

At that time in his career, Remington was still developing his craft and he often refined his field sketches with the aid of photographs by such historical photographers as Laton A. Huffman. Generally, the artist's drawings were executed in pen-and-ink and given to a professional wood-engraver who prepared the blocks for the publisher. The engraver then cut his own name or initials and the letters "sc" (symbol for engraver) into a corner of the block. Later, the engraver was eliminated when a photomechanical halftone process was developed that reproduced the watercolors the artist was perfecting.

In the years that followed, easterners visualized the Old West only as Remington portrayed it. His work became widely published, as was his prose. The painting style he developed became popular and he was acclaimed a master sculptor when he produced his first bronze, "The Bronco Buster," in 1895. His talent was such that he would surely have received acclaim eventually without the help of Roosevelt and *Century* magazine, but it would have taken longer.

While Remington climbed the ladder of success in the art world, Roosevelt became more and more involved in politics and yet, somehow, was able to find the time to become a prolific writer. He published seven books, as well as numerous articles; was appointed assistant secretary of the navy; and was one of the leaders of the Rough Riders in the charge up San Juan Hill in Cuba. At the end of the war with Spain, Roosevelt returned to find himself a hero; he was elected governor of New York State and his political career flourished.

Roosevelt was elected to the highest office in the land in 1904. Remington's bronzes and his impressionistic canvases brought him the accolades that all artists want for their work. Together, the politician and the artist created epics from the ordinary lives in the Old West. And from those adventures, the American cowboy became a hero.

Jeanne Snodgrass King
Thomas Gilcrease Institute of
American History and Art
Tulsa, Oklahoma

CONTENTS

vii

See all original Century
Mags library /HClayton

Also see
Century Mag June, 1893 "In Cowboy-Land" w/ 3 F.R. illus

CHAPTER ONE

TITLE PAGE

VOL XXXV   FEB, 1888   NO 4.

Illus by Frederic Remington.

RANCH LIFE IN THE FAR WEST

IN THE CATTLE COUNTRY

OLD-STYLE TEXAN COWMAN.

THE great grazing lands of the West lie in what is known as the arid belt, which stretches from British America on the north to Mexico on the south, through the middle of the United States. It includes New Mexico, part of Arizona, Colorado, Wyoming, Montana, and the western portion of Texas, Kansas, Nebraska, and Dakota. It must not be understood by this that more cattle are to be found here than elsewhere, for the contrary is true, it being a fact often lost sight of that the number of cattle raised on the small, thick-lying farms of the fertile Eastern States is actually many times greater than that of those scattered over the vast, barren ranches of the far West; for stock will always be most plentiful in districts where corn and other winter food can be grown. But in this arid belt, and in this arid belt only,— save in a few similar tracts on the Pacific slope,— stock-raising is almost the sole industry, except in the mountain districts where there is mining. The whole region is one vast stretch of grazing country, with only here and there spots of farm-land, in most places there being nothing more like agriculture than is implied in the cutting of some tons of wild hay or the planting of a garden patch for home use. This is especially true of the northern portion of the region, which comprises the basin of the Upper Missouri, and with which alone I am familiar. Here there are no fences to speak of, and all the land north of the Black Hills and the Big Horn Mountains and between the Rockies and the Dakota wheat-fields might be spoken of as one gigantic, unbroken pasture, where cowboys and branding-irons take the place of fences.

The country throughout this great Upper Missouri basin has a wonderful sameness of character; and the rest of the arid belt, lying to the southward, is closely akin to it in its main features. A traveler seeing it for the first time is especially struck by its look of parched, barren desolation; he can with difficulty believe that it will support cattle at all. It is a region of light rainfall; the grass is short and comparatively scanty; there is no timber except along the beds of the streams, and in many places there are alkali deserts where nothing grows but sage-brush and cactus. Now the land stretches out into level, seemingly endless plains or into rolling prairies; again it is broken by abrupt hills and deep, winding valleys; or else it is crossed by chains of buttes, usually bare, but often clad with a dense growth of dwarfed pines or gnarled, stunted cedars. The muddy rivers run in broad, shallow beds, which after heavy rainfalls are filled to the brim by the swollen torrents, while in droughts the larger streams dwindle into sluggish trickles of clearer water, and the smaller ones dry up entirely, but in occasional deep pools.

All through the region, except on the great

1

Indian reservation, there has been a scanty and sparse settlement, quite peculiar in its character. In the forest the woodchopper comes first; on the fertile prairies the granger is the pioneer; but on the long stretching uplands of the far West it is the men who guard and follow the horned herds that prepare the way for the settlers who come after. The high plains of the Upper Missouri and its tributary rivers were first opened, and are still held, by the stockmen, and the whole civilization of the region has received the stamp of their marked and individual characteristics. They were from the South, not from the East, although many men from the latter region came out along the great transcontinental railway lines and joined them in their northern migration.

They were not dwellers in towns, and from the nature of their industry lived as far apart from each other as possible. In choosing new ranges, old cow-hands, who are also seasoned plainsmen, are invariably sent ahead, perhaps a year in advance, to spy out the land and pick the best places. One of these may go by himself, or more often, especially if they have to penetrate little known or entirely unknown tracts, two or three will go together, the owner or manager of the herd himself being one of them. Perhaps their herds may already be on the border of the wild and uninhabited country: in that case they may have to take but a few days' journey before finding the stretches of sheltered, long-grass land that they seek. For instance, when I wished to move my own elkhorn steer brand on to a new ranch I had to spend barely a week in traveling north among the Little Missouri Bad Lands before finding what was then untrodden ground far outside the range of any of my neighbors' cattle. But if a large outfit is going to shift its quarters it must go much farther; and both the necessity and the

2

AN EXPLORING OUTFIT.

AN EPISODE IN THE OPENING UP OF A CATTLE COUNTRY.

3

THE MIDDAY MEAL.

chance for long wanderings were especially great when the final overthrow of the northern Horse Indians opened the whole Upper Missouri basin at one sweep to the stockmen. Then the advance-guards or explorers, each on one horse and leading another with food and bedding, were often absent months at a time, threading their way through the trackless wastes of plain, plateau, and riverbottom. If possible they would choose a country that would be good for winter and summer alike; but often this could not be done, and then they would try to find a well-watered tract on which the cattle could be summered, and from which they could be driven in fall to their sheltered winter range—for the cattle in winter eat snow, and an entirely waterless region, if broken, and with good pasturage, is often the best possible winter ground, as it is sure not to have been eaten off at all during the summer, while in the bottom the grass is always cropped down soonest. Many outfits regularly shift their herds every spring and fall; but with us in the Bad Lands all we do, when cold weather sets in, is to drive our beasts off the scantily grassed river-bottom

back ten miles or more among the broken buttes and plateaux of the uplands to where the brown hay, cured on the stalk, stands thick in the winding *coulées.*

These lookouts or forerunners having returned, the herds are set in motion as early in the spring as may be, so as to get on the ground in time to let the travel-worn beasts rest and gain flesh before winter sets in. Each herd is accompanied by a dozen, or a score, or a couple of score, of cowboys, according to its size, and beside it rumble and jolt the heavy four-horse wagons that hold the food and bedding of the men and the few implements they will need at the end of their journey. As long as possible they follow the trails made by the herds that have already traveled in the same direction, and when these end they strike out for themselves. In the Upper Missouri basin, the pioneer herds soon had to scatter out and each find its own way among the great dreary solitudes, creeping carefully along so that the cattle might not be overdriven and might have water at the halting-places. An outfit might thus be months on its lonely journey, slowly making its way

4

over melancholy, pathless plains, or down the valleys of the lonely rivers. It was tedious, harassing work, as the weary cattle had to be driven carefully and quietly during the day and strictly guarded at night, with a perpetual watch kept for Indians or white horse-thieves. Often they would skirt the edges of the streams for days at a time, seeking for a ford or a good swimming crossing, and if the water was up and the quicksand deep the danger to the riders was serious and the risk of loss among the cattle very great.

At last, after days of excitement and danger and after months of weary, monotonous toil, the chosen ground is reached and the

by several yoke of oxen, or perhaps by six or eight mules. To guard against the numerous mishaps of prairie travel, two or three of these prairie schooners usually go together, the brawny teamsters, known either as "bull-whackers" or as "mule-skinners," stalking beside their slow-moving teams.

The small outlying camps are often tents, or mere dug-outs in the ground. But at the main ranch there will be a cluster of log buildings, including a separate cabin for the foreman or ranchman; often another in which to cook and eat; a long house for the men to sleep in; stables, sheds, a blacksmith's shop, etc.,— the whole group forming quite a little settle-

THE OUTLYING CAMP.

final camp pitched. The footsore animals are turned loose to shift for themselves, outlying camps of two or three men each being established to hem them in. Meanwhile the primitive ranch-house, out-buildings, and corrals are built, the unhewn cottonwood logs being chinked with moss and mud, while the roofs are of branches covered with dirt, spades and axes being the only tools needed for the work. Bunks, chairs, and tables are all home-made, and as rough as the houses they are in. The supplies of coarse, rude food are carried perhaps two or three hundred miles from the nearest town, either in the ranch-wagons or else by some regular freighting outfit, whose huge canvas-topped prairie schooners are each drawn

ment, with the corrals, the stacks of natural hay, and the patches of fenced land for gardens or horse pastures. This little settlement may be situated right out in the treeless, nearly level open, but much more often is placed in the partly wooded bottom of a creek or river, sheltered by the usual background of somber brown hills.

When the northern plains began to be settled, such a ranch would at first be absolutely alone in the wilderness, but others of the same sort were sure soon to be established within twenty or thirty miles on one side or the other. The lives of the men in such places were strangely cut off from the outside world, and, indeed, the same is true to a

5

hardly less extent at the present day. Sometimes the wagons are sent for provisions, and the beef-steers are at stated times driven off for shipment. Parties of hunters and trappers call now and then. More rarely small bands of emigrants go by in search of new homes, impelled by the restless, aimless craving for change so deeply grafted in the breast of the American borderer: the white-topped wagons are loaded with domestic goods, with sallow, dispirited-looking women, and with tow-headed children; while the gaunt, moody frontiermen slouch alongside, rifle on shoulder, lank, homely, uncouth, and yet with a curious suggestion of grim strength underlying it all. Or cowboys from neighboring ranches will ride over, looking for lost horses, or seeing if their cattle have strayed off the range. But this is all. Civilization seems as remote as if we were living in an age long past. The whole existence is patriarchal in character: it is the life of men who live in the open, who tend their herds on horseback, who go armed and ready to guard their lives by their own prowess, whose wants are very simple, and who call no man master. Ranching is an occupation like those of vigorous, primitive pastoral peoples, having little in common with the humdrum, workaday business world of the nineteenth century; and the free ranchman in his manner of life shows more kinship to an Arab sheik than to a sleek city merchant or tradesman.

By degrees the country becomes what in a stock-raising region passes for well settled. In addition to the great ranches smaller ones are established, with a few hundred, or even a few score, head of cattle apiece; and now and then miserable farmers straggle in to fight a losing and desperate battle with drought, cold, and grasshoppers. The wheels of the heavy wagons, driven always over the same course from one ranch to another, or to the remote frontier towns from which they get their goods, wear ruts in the soil, and roads are soon formed, perhaps originally following the deep trails made by the vanished buffalo. These roads lead down the river-bottoms or along the crests of the divides or else strike out fairly across the prairie, and a man may sometimes travel a hundred miles along one without coming to a house or camp of any sort. If they lead to a shipping point whence the beeves are sent to market, the cattle, traveling in single file, will have worn many and deep paths on each side of the wheel-marks; and the roads between important places which are regularly used either by the United States Government, by stage-coach lines, or by freight teams become deeply worn landmarks — as, for instance, near us, the Deadwood and the old Fort Keogh trails.

Cattle-ranching can only be carried on in its present form while the population is scanty; and so in stock-raising regions, pure and simple, there are usually few towns, and these are almost always at the shipping points for cattle. But, on the other hand, wealthy cattlemen, like miners who have done well, always spend their money freely; and accordingly towns like Denver, Cheyenne, and Helena, where these two classes are the most influential in the community, are far pleasanter places of residence than cities of five times their population in the exclusively agricultural States to the eastward.

A true "cow town" is worth seeing, — such a one as Miles City, for instance, especially at the time of the annual meeting of the great Montana Stock-raisers' Association. Then the whole place is full to overflowing, the importance of the meeting and the fun of the attendant frolics, especially the horse-races, drawing from the surrounding ranch country many hundreds of men of every degree, from the rich stock-owner worth his millions to the ordinary cowboy who works for forty dollars a month. It would be impossible to imagine a more typically American assemblage, for although there are always a certain number of foreigners, usually English, Irish, or German, yet they have become completely Americanized; and on the whole it would be difficult to gather a finer body of men, in spite of their numerous shortcomings. The ranch-owners differ more from each other than do the cowboys; and the former certainly compare very favorably with similar classes of capitalists in the East. Anything more foolish than the demagogic outcry against "cattle kings" it would be difficult to imagine. Indeed, there are very few businesses so absolutely legitimate as stock-raising and so beneficial to the nation at large; and a successful stock-grower must not only be shrewd, thrifty, patient, and enterprising, but he must also possess qualities of personal bravery, hardihood, and self-reliance to a degree not demanded in the least by any mercantile occupation in a community long settled. Stockmen are in the West the pioneers of civilization, and their daring and adventurousness make the after settlement of the region possible. The whole country owes them a great debt.

The most successful ranchmen are those, usually South-westerners, who have been bred to the business and have grown up with it; but many Eastern men, including not a few college graduates, have also done excellently by devoting their whole time and energy to their work, — although Easterners who invest their money in cattle without knowing anything of the business, or who trust all to their subordinates, are naturally enough likely to incur heavy losses. Stockmen are learning more and more to act together; and certainly the meetings of their associations are conducted with a dignity and good sense that would do credit to any parliamentary body.

during their long drives with every kind of team, through every kind of country, and in every kind of weather, who, proud of their really wonderful skill as reinsmen and conscious of their high standing in any frontier community, look down on and sneer at the plodding teamsters; trappers and wolfers, whose business is to poison wolves, with shaggy, knock-kneed

A ROW IN A CATTLE TOWN.

But the cowboys resemble one another much more and outsiders much less than is the case even with their employers, the ranchmen. A town in the cattle country, when for some cause it is thronged with men from the neighborhood round about, always presents a picturesque sight on the wooden sidewalks of the broad, dusty streets. The men who ply the various industries known only to frontier existence jostle one another as they saunter to and fro or lounge lazily in front of the straggling, cheap-looking board houses: hunters, in their buckskin shirts and fur caps, greasy and unkempt, but with resolute faces and sullen, watchful eyes, that are ever on the alert; teamsters, surly and self-contained, with slouch hats and great cowhide boots; stage-drivers, their faces seamed by hardship and exposure

ponies to carry their small bales and bundles of furs — beaver, wolf, fox, and occasionally otter; silent sheep-herders, with cast-down faces, never able to forget the absolute solitude and monotony of their dreary lives, nor to rid their minds of the thought of the woolly idiots they pass all their days in tending,— these are the men who have come to town, either on business or else to frequent the flaunting saloons and gaudy hells of all kinds in search of the coarse, vicious excitement that in the minds of many of them does duty as pleasure, the only form of pleasure they have ever had a chance to know. Indians too, wrapped in blankets and with stolid, emotionless faces, stalk silently round among the whites, or join in the gambling and horse-racing. If the town is on the borders of the

7

mountain country, there will also be sinewy lumbermen, rough-looking miners and packers, whose business it is to guide the long mule trains that go where wagons can not and whose work in packing needs special and peculiar skill; and mingled with and drawn from all these classes are desperadoes of every grade, from the gambler up through the horse-thief to the murderous professional bully, or, as he is locally called, "bad man"—now, however, a much less conspicuous object than formerly.

But everywhere among these plainsmen and mountain-men, and more important than any, are the cowboys,—the men who follow the calling that has brought such towns into being. Singly, or in twos or threes, they gallop their wiry little horses down the street, their lithe, supple figures erect or swaying slightly as they sit loosely in the saddle; while their stirrups are so long that their knees are hardly bent, the bridles not taut enough to keep the chains from clanking. They are smaller and less muscular than the wielders of ax and pick; but they are as hardy and self-reliant as any men who ever breathed — with bronzed, set faces, and keen eyes that look all the world straight in the face without flinching as they flash out from under the broad-brimmed hats. Peril and hardship, and years of long toil broken by weeks of brutal dissipation, draw haggard lines across their eager faces, but never dim their reckless eyes nor break their bearing of defiant self-confidence. They do not walk well, partly because they so rarely do any work out of the saddle, partly because their *chaperajos* or leather overalls hamper them when on the ground; but their appearance is striking for all that, and picturesque too, with their jingling spurs, the big revolvers stuck in their belts, and bright silk handkerchiefs knotted loosely round their necks over the open collars of the flannel shirts. When drunk on the villainous whisky of the frontier towns, they cut mad antics, riding their horses into the saloons, firing their pistols right and left, from boisterous light-heartedness rather than from any viciousness, and indulging too often in deadly shooting affrays, brought on either by the accidental contact of the moment or on account of some long-standing grudge, or perhaps because of bad blood between two ranches or localities; but except while on such sprees they are quiet, rather self-contained men, perfectly frank and simple, and on their own ground treat a stranger with the most whole-souled hospitality, doing all in their power for him and scorning to take any reward in return. Although prompt to resent an injury, they are not at all apt to be rude to outsiders, treating them with what can almost be called a grave courtesy. They are

much better fellows and pleasanter companions than small farmers or agricultural laborers; nor are the mechanics and workmen of a great city to be mentioned in the same breath.

The bulk of the cowboys themselves are South-westerners; but there are also many from the Eastern and the Northern States, who if they begin young do quite as well as the Southerner. The best hands are fairly bred to the work and follow it from their youth up. Nothing can be more foolish than for an Easterner to think he can become a cowboy in a few months' time. Many a young fellow comes out hot with enthusiasm for life on the plains, only to learn that his clumsiness is greater than he could have believed possible; that the cowboy business is like any other and has to be learned by serving a painful apprenticeship; and that this apprenticeship implies the endurance of rough fare, hard living, dirt, exposure of every kind, no little toil, and month after month of the dullest monotony. For cowboy work there is need of special traits and special training, and young Easterners should be sure of themselves before trying it: the struggle for existence is very keen in the far West, and it is no place for men who lack the ruder, coarser virtues and physical qualities, no matter how intellectual or how refined and delicate their sensibilities. Such are more likely to fail there than in older communities. Probably during the past few years more than half of the young Easterners who have come West with a little money to learn the cattle business have failed signally and lost what they had in the beginning. The West, especially the far West, needs men who have been bred on the farm or in the workshop far more than it does clerks or college graduates.

Some of the cowboys are Mexicans, who generally do the actual work well enough, but are not trustworthy; moreover, they are always regarded with extreme disfavor by the Texans in an outfit, among whom the intolerant caste spirit is very strong. Southern-born whites will never work under them, and look down upon all colored or half-caste races. One spring I had with my wagon a Pueblo Indian, an excellent rider and roper, but a drunken, worthless, lazy devil; and in the summer of 1886 there were with us a Sioux half-breed, a quiet, hard-working, faithful fellow, and a mulatto, who was one of the best cow-hands in the whole round-up.

Cowboys, like most Westerners, occasionally show remarkable versatility in their tastes and pursuits. One whom I know has abandoned his regular occupation for the past nine months, during which time he has been in succession a bartender, a school-teacher,

COWBOY FUN.

and a probate judge! Another, whom I once employed for a short while, had passed through even more varied experiences, including those of a barber, a sailor, an apothecary, and a buffalo-hunter.

As a rule the cowboys are known to each other only by their first names, with, perhaps, as a prefix, the title of the brand for which they are working. Thus I remember once over-hearing a casual remark to the effect that "Bar Y Harry" had married "the seven Open A girl," the latter being the daughter of a neighboring ranchman. Often they receive nicknames, as, for instance, Dutch Wan-nigan, Windy Jack, and Kid Williams, all of whom are on the list of my personal acquaint-ances.

No man traveling through or living in the country need fear molestation from the cow-boys unless he himself accompanies them on their drinking-bouts, or in other ways plays the fool, for they are, with us at any rate, very good fellows, and the most determined and effective foes of real law-breakers, such as horse and cattle thieves, murderers, etc. Few of the outrages quoted in Eastern papers as their handiwork are such in reality, the average Easterner apparently considering every indi-vidual who wears a broad hat and carries a six-shooter a cowboy. These outrages are, as

9

IN A BOG-HOLE.

a rule, the work of the roughs and criminals who always gather on the outskirts of civilization and who infest every frontier town until the decent citizens become sufficiently numerous and determined to take the law into their own hands and drive them out. The old buffalo-hunters, who formed a distinct class, became powerful forces for evil once they had destroyed the vast herds of mighty beasts whose pursuit had been their means of livelihood. They were absolutely shiftless and improvident; they had no settled habits; they were inured to peril and hardship, but entirely unaccustomed to steady work; and so they afforded just the materials from which to make the bolder and more desperate kinds of criminals. When the game was gone they hung round the settlements for some little time, and then many of them naturally took to horse-stealing, cattle-killing, and highway robbery, although others, of course, went into honest pursuits. They were men who died off rapidly, however; for it is curious to see how many of these plainsmen, in spite of their iron nerves and thews, have their constitutions completely undermined, as much by the terrible hardships they have endured as by the fits of prolonged and bestial revelry with which they have varied them.

The "bad men," or professional fighters and man-killers, are of a different stamp, quite a number of them being, according to their light, perfectly honest. These are the men who do most of the killing in frontier communities; yet it is a noteworthy fact that the men who are killed generally deserve their fate. These men are, of course, used to brawling, and are not only sure shots, but, what is equally important, able to "draw" their weapons with marvelous quickness. They think nothing whatever of murder, and are the dread and terror of their associates; yet they are very chary of taking the life of a man of good standing, and will often weaken and back down at once if confronted fearlessly. With many of them their courage arises from confidence in their own powers and knowledge of the fear in which they are held; and men of this type often show the white feather when they get in a tight place. Others, however, will face any odds without flinching. On the other hand, I have known of these men fighting, when mortally wounded, with a cool, ferocious despair that was terrible. As elsewhere, so here, very quiet men are often those who in an emergency show themselves best able to hold their own. These desperadoes always try to "get the drop" on a foe — that is, to take him at a disadvantage before he can use his own weapon. I have known more men killed in this way, when the affair was wholly one-sided, than I have known to be shot in fair fight; and I have known fully as many who were shot by accident. It is wonderful, in the

10

event of a street-fight, how few bullets seem to hit the men they are aimed at.

During the last two or three years the stockmen have united to put down all these dangerous characters, often by the most summary exercise of lynch law. Notorious bullies and murderers have been taken out and hung, while the bands of horse and cattle thieves have been regularly hunted down and destroyed in pitched fights by parties of armed

PULLING A COW OUT OF THE MUD.

cowboys; and as a consequence most of our territory is now perfectly law-abiding. One such fight occurred north of me early last spring. The horse-thieves were overtaken on the banks of the Missouri; two of their number were slain, and the others were driven on the ice, which broke, and two more were drowned. A few months previously another gang, whose headquarters were near the Canadian line, were surprised in their hut; two or three were shot down by the cowboys as they tried to come out, while the rest barricaded themselves in and fought until the great log-hut was set on fire, when they broke forth in a body, and nearly all were killed at once, only one or two making their escape. A little over a year ago one committee of vigilantes in east-

ern Montana shot or hung nearly sixty — not, however, with the best judgment in all cases.

A stranger in the North-western cattle country is especially struck by the resemblance the settlers show in their pursuits and habits to the Southern people. Nebraska and Dakota, east of the Missouri, resemble Minnesota and Iowa and the States farther east, but Montana and the Dakota cow country show more kinship with Texas; for while elsewhere in America settlement has advanced along the parallels of latitude, on the great plains it has followed the meridians of longitude and has gone northerly rather than westerly. The business is carried on as it is in the South. The rough-rider of the plains, the hero of rope and revolver, is first cousin to the backwoodsman of the southern Alleghanies, the man of the ax and the rifle; he is only a unique offshoot of the frontier stock of the South-west. The very term "round-up" is used by the cowboys in the exact sense in which it is employed by the hill people and mountaineers of Kentucky, Tennessee, and North Carolina, with whom also labor is dear and poor land cheap, and whose few cattle are consequently branded and turned loose in the woods exactly as is done with the great herds on the plains.

But the ranching industry itself was copied from the Mexicans, of whose land and herds the South-western frontiermen of Texas took forcible possession; and the traveler in the North-west will see at a glance that the terms and practices of our business are largely of Spanish origin. The cruel curb-bit and heavy stock-saddle, with its high horn and cantle, prove that we have adopted Spanish-American horse-gear; and the broad hat, huge blunt spurs, and leather *chaperajos* of the rider, as well as the corral in which the stock are penned, all alike show the same ancestry. Throughout the cattle country east of the Rocky Mountains, from the Rio Grande to the Saskatch-

11

ewan, the same terms are in use and the same system is followed; but on the Pacific slope, in California, there are certain small differences, even in nomenclature. Thus, we of the great plains all use the double *cincha* saddle, with one girth behind the horse's fore legs and another farther back, while Californians prefer one with a single *cincha*, which seems to us much inferior for stock-work. Again, Californians use the Spanish word "lasso," which with us has been entirely dropped, no plainsman with pre-

or quite as highly as good horsemanship, and is much rarer. Once a cowboy is a good roper and rider, the only other accomplishment he values is skill with his great army revolver, it being taken for granted that he is already a thorough plainsman and has long mastered the details of cattle-work; for the best roper and rider alive is of little use unless he is hard-working, honest, keenly alive to his employer's interest, and very careful in the management of the cattle.

A DISPUTE OVER A BRAND.

tensions to the title thinking of any word but "rope," either as noun or verb.

The rope, whether leather lariat or made of grass, is the one essential feature of every cowboy's equipment. Loosely coiled, it hangs from the horn or is tied to one side of the saddle in front of the thigh, and is used for every conceivable emergency, a twist being taken round the stout saddle-horn the second the noose settles over the neck or around the legs of a chased animal. In helping pull a wagon up a steep pitch, in dragging an animal by the horns out of a bog-hole, in hauling up logs for the fire, and in a hundred other ways aside from its legitimate purpose, the rope is of invaluable service, and dexterity with it is prized almost

All cowboys can handle the rope with more or less ease and precision, but great skill in its use is only attained after long practice, and for its highest development needs that the man should have begun in earliest infancy. A really first-class roper can command his own price, and is usually fit for little but his own special work.

It is much the same with riding. The cowboy is an excellent rider in his own way, but his way differs from that of a trained school horseman or cross-country fox-hunter as much as it does from the horsemanship of an Arab or of a Sioux Indian, and, as with all these, it has its special merits and special defects — schoolman, fox-hunter, cowboy, Arab, and

12

Indian being all alike admirable riders in their respective styles, and each cherishing the same profound and ignorant contempt for every method but his own. The flash riders, or horse-breakers, always called "bronco busters," can perform really marvelous feats, riding with ease the most vicious and unbroken beasts, that no ordinary cowboy would dare to tackle. Although sitting seemingly so loose in the saddle, such a rider can not be jarred out of it by the wildest plunger, it being a favorite feat to sit out the antics of a bucking horse with silver half-dollars under each knee or in the stirrups under each foot. But their method of breaking is very rough, consisting only in saddling and bridling a beast by main force and then riding him, also by main force, until he is exhausted, when he is turned over as "broken." Later on the cowboy himself may train his horse to stop or wheel instantly at a touch of the reins or bit, to start at top speed at a signal, and to stand motionless when left. An intelligent pony soon picks up a good deal of knowledge about the cow business on his own account.

All cattle are branded, usually on the hip, shoulder, and side, or on any one of them, with letters, numbers, or figures, in every combination, the outfit being known by its brand. Near me, for instance, are the Three Sevens, the Thistle, the Bellows, the OX, the VI., the Seventy-six Bar (⁷⁶), and the Quarter Circle Diamond (◇) outfits. The dew-lap and the ears may also be cut, notched, or slit. All brands are registered, and are thus protected against imitators, any man tampering with them being punished as severely as possible. Unbranded animals are called *mavericks*, and when found on the round-up are either branded by the owner of the range on which they are, or else are sold for the benefit of the association. At every shipping point, as well as where the beef cattle are received, there are stock inspectors who jealously examine all the brands on the live animals or on the hides of the slaughtered ones, so as to detect any foul play, which is immediately reported to the association. It becomes second nature with a cowboy to inspect and note the brands of every bunch of animals he comes across.

Perhaps the thing that seems strangest to the traveler who for the first time crosses the bleak plains of this Upper Missouri grazing country is the small number of cattle seen. He can hardly believe he is in the great stock region, where for miles upon miles he will not see a single head, and will then come only upon a straggling herd of a few score. As a matter of fact, where there is no artificial food put up for winter use cattle always need a good deal of ground per head; and this is peculiarly the case with us in the North-west, where much of the ground is bare of vegetation and where what pasture there is is both short and sparse. It is a matter of absolute necessity, where beasts are left to shift for themselves in the open during the bitter winter weather, that they then should have grass that they have not cropped too far down; and to insure this it is necessary with us to allow on the average about twenty-five acres of ground to each animal. This means that a range of country ten miles square will keep between two and three thousand head of stock only, and if more are put on, it is at the risk of seeing a severe winter kill off half or three-quarters of the whole number. So a range may be in reality overstocked when to an Eastern and unpracticed eye it seems hardly to have on it a number worth taking into account.

Overstocking is the great danger threatening the stock-raising industry on the plains. This industry has only risen to be of more than local consequence during the past score of years, as before that time it was confined to Texas and California; but during these two decades of its existence the stockmen in different localities have again and again suffered the most ruinous losses, usually with overstocking as the ultimate cause. In the south the drought, and in the north the deep snows, and everywhere unusually bad winters, do immense damage; still, if the land is fitted for stock at all, they will, averaging one year with another, do very well so long as the feed is not cropped down too close.

But, of course, no amount of feed will make some countries worth anything for cattle that are not housed during the winter; and stockmen in choosing new ranges for their herds pay almost as much attention to the capacity of the land for yielding shelter as they do to the abundant and good quality of the grass. High up among the foot-hills of the mountains cattle will not live through the winter; and an open, rolling prairie land of heavy rainfall, and where in consequence the snow lies deep and there is no protection from the furious cold winds, is useless for winter grazing, no matter how thick and high the feed. The three essentials for a range are grass, water, and shelter: the water is only needed in summer and the shelter in winter, while it may be doubted if drought during the hot months has ever killed off more cattle than have died in consequence of exposure on shelterless ground to the icy weather, lasting from November to April.

The finest summer range may be valueless either on account of its lack of shelter or because it is in a region of heavy snowfall — portions of territory lying in the same latitude

13

14

BRONCO BUSTERS SADDLING.

and not very far apart often differing widely in this respect. This loss, of course, had nothing to do with overstocking; and the same was true of the loss that visited the few herds which spent the very hard winter of 1880 on the northern cattle plains. These were the pioneers of their kind, and the grass was all that could be desired; yet the extraordinary severity of the weather proved too much for the cattle. This was especially the case with those herds consisting of "pilgrims," as they are called—that is, of animals driven up on to the range from the south, and therefore in poor condition. One such herd of pilgrims on the Powder River suffered a loss of thirty-six hundred out of a total of four thousand, and the survivors kept alive only by browsing on the tops of cottonwoods felled for them. Even seasoned animals fared very badly. One great herd in the Yellowstone Valley lost about a fourth of its number, the loss falling mainly on the breeding cows, calves, and bulls,—always the chief sufferers, as the steers, and also the dry cows, will get through almost anything. The loss here would have been far heavier than it was had it not been for a curious trait shown by the cattle. They kept in bands of several hundred each, and during the time of the deep snows a band would make a start and travel several miles in a straight line, plowing their way through the drifts and beating out a broad track; then, when stopped by a frozen watercourse or chain of buttes, they would turn back and graze over the trail thus made, the only place where they could get at the grass.

A drenching rain, followed by a severe snap of cold, is even more destructive than deep snow, for the saturated coats of the poor beasts are turned into sheets of icy mail, and the grass-blades, frozen at the roots as well as above, change into sheaves of brittle spears as uneatable as so many icicles. Entire herds have perished in consequence of such a storm. Mere cold, however, will kill only very weak animals, which is fortunate for us, as the spirit in the thermometer during winter often sinks to fifty degrees below zero, the cold being literally arctic; yet though the cattle become thin during such a snap of weather, and sometimes have their ears, tails, and even horns frozen off, they nevertheless rarely die from the cold alone. But if there is a blizzard blowing in at such a time, the cattle need shelter, and if caught in the open, will travel for scores of miles before the storm, until they reach a break in the ground, or some stretch of dense woodland, which will shield them from the blasts. If cattle traveling in this manner come to some obstacle that they can not pass, as, for instance, a wire fence or a steep railway embankment,

they will not try to make their way back against the storm, but will simply stand with their tails to it until they drop dead in their tracks; and, accordingly, in some parts of the country—but luckily far to the south of us—the railways are fringed with countless skeletons of beasts that have thus perished, while many of the long wire fences make an almost equally bad showing. In some of the very open country of Kansas and Indian Territory, many of the herds during the past two years have suffered a loss of from sixty to eighty per cent., although this was from a variety of causes, including drought as well as severe winter weather. Too much rain is quite as bad as too little, especially if it falls after the 1st of August, for then, though the growth of grass is very rank and luxuriant, it yet has little strength and does not cure well on the stalk; and it is only possible to winter cattle at large at all because of the way in which the grass turns into natural hay by this curing on the stalk.

But scantiness of food, due to overstocking, is the one really great danger to us in the north, who do not have to fear the droughts that occasionally devastate portions of the southern ranges. In a fairly good country, if the feed is plenty, the natural increase of a herd is sure shortly to repair any damage that may be done by an unusually severe winter—unless, indeed, the latter should be one such as occurs but two or three times in a century. When, however, the grass becomes cropped down, then the loss in even an ordinary year is heavy among the weaker animals, and if the winter is at all severe it becomes simply appalling. The snow covers the shorter grass much quicker, and even when there is enough, the cattle, weak and unfit to travel around, have to work hard to get it by exertion tending to enfeeble them and render them less able to cope with the exposure and cold. Again, the grass is, of course, soonest eaten off where there is shelter; and, accordingly, the broken ground to which the animals cling during winter may be grazed bare of vegetation though the open plains, to which only the hardiest will at this season stray, may have plenty; and insufficiency of food, although not such as actually to starve them, weakens them so that they succumb readily to the cold or to one of the numerous accidents to which they are liable—as slipping off an icy butte or getting cast in a frozen washout. The cows in calf are those that suffer most, and so heavy is the loss among these and so light the calf crop that it is yet an open question whether our northern ranges are as a whole fitted for breeding. When the animals get weak they will huddle into some nook or corner or empty hut and simply stay there till they die.

15

Overstocking may cause little or no harm for two or three years, but sooner or later there comes a winter which means ruin to the ranches that have too many cattle on them; and in our country, which is even now getting crowded, it is merely a question of time as to when a winter will come that will understock the ranges by the summary process of killing off about half of all the cattle throughout the North-west

In our northern country we have "free grass"; that is, the stockmen rarely own more than small portions of the land over which their cattle range, the bulk of it being unsurveyed and still the property of the National Government—for the latter refuses to sell the soil except in small lots, acting on the wise principle of distributing it among as many owners as possible. Here and there some ranchman has acquired title to narrow strips of territory peculiarly valuable as giving water-right; but the amount of land thus occupied is small with us,—although the reverse is the case farther south,—and there is practically no fencing to speak of. As a consequence, the land is one vast pasture, and the man who overstocks his own range damages his neighbors as much as himself. These huge northern pastures are too dry and the soil too poor to be used for agriculture until the rich, wet lands to the east and west are occupied; and at present we have little fear from grangers. Of course, in the end much of the ground will be taken up for small farms, but the farmers that so far have come in have absolutely failed to make even a living, except now and then by raising a few vegetables for the use of the stockmen; and we are inclined to welcome the incoming of an occasional settler, if he is a decent man, especially as, by the laws of the Territories in which the great grazing plains lie, he is obliged to fence in his own patch of cleared ground, and we do not have to keep our cattle out of it.

At present we are far more afraid of each other. There are always plenty of men who for the sake of the chance of gain they themselves run are willing to jeopardize the interests of their neighbors by putting on more cattle than the land will support—for the loss, of course, falls as heavily on the man who has put on the right number as on him who has put on too many; and it is against these individuals that we have to guard so far as we are able. To protect ourselves completely is impossible, but the very identity of interest that renders all of us liable to suffer for the fault of a few also renders us as a whole able to take some rough measures to guard against the wrong-doing of a portion of our number; for the fact that the cattle wander intermixed over the ranges forces all the ranchmen of a locality to combine if they wish to do their work effectively. Accordingly, the stockmen of a neighborhood, when it holds as many cattle as it safely can, usually unitedly refuse to work with any one who puts in another herd. In the cow country a man is peculiarly dependent upon his neighbors, and a small outfit is wholly unable to work without their assistance when once the cattle have mingled completely with those of other brands. A large outfit is much more master of its destiny, and can do its own work quite by itself; but even such a one can be injured in countless ways if the hostility of the neighboring ranchmen is incurred. So a certain check is put to undue crowding of the ranges; but it is only partial.

The best days of ranching are over; and though there are many ranchmen who still make money, yet during the past two or three years the majority have certainly lost. This is especially true of the numerous Easterners who went into the business without any experience and trusted themselves entirely to their Western representatives; although, on the other hand, many of those who have made most money at it are Easterners, who, however, have happened to be naturally fitted for the work and who have deliberately settled down to learning the business as they would have learned any other, devoting their whole time and energy to it. As the country grows older, stock-raising will in some places die out, and in others entirely change its character; the ranches will be broken up, will be gradually modified into stock-farms, or, if on good soil, may even fall under the sway of the husbandman.

In its present form stock-raising on the plains is doomed, and can hardly outlast the century. The great free ranches, with their barbarous, picturesque, and curiously fascinating surroundings, mark a primitive stage of existence as surely as do the great tracts of primeval forests, and like the latter must pass away before the onward march of our people; and we who have felt the charm of the life, and have exulted in its abounding vigor and its bold, restless freedom, will not only regret its passing for our own sakes only, but must also feel real sorrow that those who come after us are not to see, as we have seen, what is perhaps the pleasantest, healthiest, and most exciting phase of American existence.

Theodore Roosevelt.

16

CHAPTER TWO

VOL XXXV   March, 1888   No. 5.

THE HOME RANCH

A MONTANA TYPE.

MY home ranch lies on both sides of the Little Missouri, the nearest ranchman above me being about twelve, and the nearest below me about ten, miles distant. The general course of the stream here is northerly, but, while flowing through my ranch, it takes a great westerly reach of some three miles, walled in, as always, between chains of steep, high bluffs half a mile or more apart. The stream twists down through the valley in long sweeps, leaving oval wooded bottoms, first on one side and then on the other; and in an open glade among the thick-growing timber stands the long, low house of hewn logs.

Just in front of the ranch veranda is a line of old cottonwoods that shade it during the fierce heats of summer, rendering it always cool and pleasant. But a few feet beyond these trees comes the cut-off bank of the river, through whose broad, sandy bed the shallow stream winds as if lost, except when a freshet fills it from brim to brim with foaming yellow water. The bluffs that wall in the river-valley curve back in semicircles, rising from its alluvial bottom generally as abrupt cliffs, but often as steep, grassy slopes that lead up to great level plateaus; and the line is broken every mile or two by the entrance of a coulée, or dry creek, whose head branches may be twenty miles back. Above us, where the river comes round the bend, the valley is very narrow, and the high buttes bounding it rise, sheer and barren, into scalped hill-peaks and naked knife-blade ridges.

The other buildings stand in the same open glade with the ranch house, the dense growth of cottonwoods and matted, thorny underbrush making a wall all about, through which we have chopped our wagon roads and trodden out our own bridle-paths. The cattle have now trampled down this brush a little, but deer still lie in it, only a couple of hundred yards from the house; and from the door sometimes in the evening one can see them peer out into the open, or make their way down, timidly and cautiously, to drink at the river. The stable, sheds, and other outbuildings, with the hayricks and the pens for such cattle as we bring in during winter, are near the house; the patch of fenced garden land is on the edge of the woods; and near the middle of the glade stands the high, circular horse-corral, with a snubbing-post in the center, and a wing built out from one side of the gate entrance, so that the saddle band can be driven in without trouble. As it is very hard to work cattle where there is much brush, the larger cow-corral is some four miles off on an open bottom.

A ranchman's life is certainly a very pleasant one, albeit generally varied with plenty of hardship and anxiety. Although occasionally he passes days of severe toil,—for example, if he goes on the round-up he works as hard as any of his men,—yet he no longer

17

has to undergo the monotonous drudgery attendant upon the tasks of the cowboy or of the apprentice in the business. His fare is simple; but, if he chooses, it is good enough. Many ranches are provided with nothing at all but salt pork, canned goods, and bread; indeed, it is a curious fact that in traveling through this cow country it is often impossible to get any milk or butter; but this is only because the owners or managers are too lazy to take enough trouble to insure their own comfort. We ourselves always keep up two or three cows, choosing such as are naturally tame, and so we invariably have plenty of milk and, when there is time for churning, a good deal of butter. We also keep hens, which, in spite of the damaging inroads of hawks, bob-cats, and foxes, supply us with eggs, and in time of need, when our rifles have failed to keep us in game, with stewed, roast, or fried chicken also. From our garden we get potatoes, and unless drought, frost, or grasshoppers interfere (which they do about every second year), other vegetables as well. For fresh meat we depend chiefly upon our prowess as hunters.

During much of the time we are away on the different round-ups, that "wheeled house," the great four-horse wagon, being then our home; but when at the ranch our routine of life is always much the same, save during

the scattered groups of the saddle band, our six or eight mares, with their colts, keep by themselves, and are rarely bothered by us, as no cowboy ever rides anything but horses, because mares give great trouble where all the animals have to be herded together. Once every two or three days somebody rides round and finds out where each of these smaller bands is, but the man who goes out in the morning merely gathers one bunch. He drives these into the corral, the other men (who have been lolling idly about the house or stable, fixing their saddles or doing any odd job) coming out with their ropes as soon as they hear the patter of the unshod hoofs and the shouts of the cowboy driver. Going into the corral, and standing near the center, each of us picks out some one of his own string from among the animals that are trotting and running in a compact mass round the circle; and after one or more trials, according to his skill, ropes it and leads it out. When all have caught their horses the rest are again turned loose, together with those that have been kept up overnight. Some horses soon get tame and do not need to be roped; my pet cutting pony, little Muley, and good old Manitou, my companion in so many

ELK HORN RANCH BUILDINGS.

hunting trips, will neither of them stay with the rest of their fellows that are jamming and jostling each other as they rush round in the dust of the corral, but they very sensibly walk up and stand quietly with the men in the middle, by the snubbing-post. Both are great pets, Manitou in particular; the wise old fellow being very fond of bread and sometimes coming up of his own accord to the ranch house and even putting his head into the door to beg for it.

Once saddled, the men ride off on their different tasks; for almost everything is done in the saddle, except that in winter we cut our firewood and quarry our coal,— both on the

the excessively bitter weather of midwinter, when there is little to do except to hunt, if the days are fine enough. We breakfast early — before dawn when the nights have grown long, and rarely later than sunrise, even in midsummer. Perhaps before this meal, certainly the instant it is over, the man whose duty it is rides off to hunt up and drive in the saddle band. Each of us has his own string of horses, eight or ten in number, and the whole band usually split up into two or three companies. In addition to ranch,—and in summer attend to the garden and put up what wild hay we need.

If any horses have strayed, one or two of the men will be sent off to look for them; for hunting lost horses is one of the commonest' and most irksome of our duties. Every outfit always has certain of its horses at large; and if they remain out long enough they become

If the men do not go horse-hunting they may ride off over the range; for there is generally some work to be done among the cattle, such as driving in and branding calves that have been overlooked by the round-up, or getting some animal out of a bog-hole. During the early spring months, before the round-up begins, the chief work is in haul-

ROPING IN A HORSE-CORRAL.

as wild and wary as deer and have to be regularly surrounded and run down. On one occasion, when three of mine had been running loose for a couple of months, we had to follow at full speed for at least fifteen miles before exhausting them enough to enable us to get some control over them and head them towards a corral. Twice I have had horses absent nearly a year before they were recovered. One of them, after being on the ranch nine months, went off one night and traveled about two hundred miles in a straight line back to its old haunts, swimming the Yellowstone on the way. Two others were at one time away nearly eighteen months, during which time we saw them twice, and on one occasion a couple of the men fairly ran their horses down in following them. We began to think they were lost for good, as they were all the time going farther down towards the Sioux country, but we finally recovered them.

ing out mired cows and steers; and if we did not keep a sharp lookout, the losses at this season would be very serious. As long as everything is frozen solid there is, of course, no danger from miring; but when the thaw comes, along towards the beginning of March, a period of new danger to the cattle sets in. When the ice breaks up, the streams are left with an edging of deep bog, while the quicksand is at its worst. As the frost goes out of the soil, the ground round every little alkali-spring changes into a trembling quagmire, and deep holes of slimy, tenacious mud form in the bottom of all the gullies. The cattle, which have had to live on snow for three or four months, arc very eager for water, and are weak and in poor condition. They rush heedlessly into any pool and stand there, drinking gallons of the icy water and sinking steadily into the mud. When they try to get out they are already too deep down, and are too weak to make a pro-

19

longed struggle. After one or two fits of desperate floundering, they resign themselves to their fate with dumb apathy and are lost, unless some one of us riding about discovers and hauls them out. They may be thus lost in wonderfully small mud-holes; often they will be found dead in a gulch but two or three feet across, or in the quicksand of a creek so nar-

covered with a sun-baked crust, that let them through as if they had stepped on a trap-door. There being several of us along, we got down our ropes and dragged both unfortunates out in short order.

When the river is up it is a very common thing for a horseman to have great difficulty in crossing, for the swift, brown water runs

A DEEP FORD.

row that it could almost be jumped. An alkali-hole, where the water oozes out through the thick clay, is the worst of all, owing to the ropy tenacity with which the horrible substance sticks and clings to any unfortunate beast that gets into it.

In the spring these mud-holes cause very serious losses among the cattle, and are at all times fruitful sources of danger; indeed, during an ordinary year more cattle die from getting mired than from any other cause. In addition to this they also often prove very annoying to the rider himself, as getting his steed mired or caught in a quicksand is one of the commonest of the accidents that beset a horseman in the far West. This usually happens in fording a river, if the latter is at all high, or else in crossing one of the numerous creeks; although I once saw a horse and rider suddenly engulfed while leisurely walking over what appeared to be dry land. They had come to an alkali mud-hole, an old buffalo-wallow, which had filled up and was

over a bed of deep quicksand that is ever shifting. An inexperienced horse, or a mule, —for a mule is useless in mud or quicksand,— becomes mad with fright in such a crossing, and, after speedily exhausting its strength in wild struggles, will throw itself on its side and drown unless the rider gets it out. An old horse used to such work will, on the contrary, take matters quietly and often push along through really dangerous quicksand. Old Manitou never loses his head for an instant; but, now resting a few seconds, now feeling his way cautiously forward, and now making two or three desperate plunges, will go on wherever a horse possibly can. It is really dangerous crossing some of the creeks, as the bottom may give way where it seems hardest; and if one is alone he may work hours in vain before getting his horse out, even after taking off both saddle and bridle, the only hope being to head it so that every plunge takes it an inch or two in the right direction.

Nor are mud-holes the only danger the

horseman has to fear; for in much of the Bad Lands the buttes are so steep and broken that it needs genuine mountaineering skill to get through them, and no horse but a Western one, bred to the business, could accomplish the feat. In many parts of our country it is impossible for a horseman who does not know the land to cross it, and it is difficult enough even for an experienced hand. For a stretch of nearly ten miles along the Little Missouri above my range, and where it passes through it, there are but three or four places where it is possible for a horseman to get out to the eastern prairie through the exceedingly broken country lying back from the river. In places this very rough ground comes down to the water; elsewhere it lies back near the heads of the creeks. In such very bad ground the whole country seems to be one tangled chaos of cañon-like valleys, winding gullies, and washouts, with abrupt, unbroken sides, isolated peaks of sandstone, marl, or "gumbo" clay, which rain turns into slippery glue, and hill chains whose ridges always end in sheer cliffs. After a man has made his way with infinite toil for half a mile, a point will be reached around which it is an absolute impossibility to go, and the adventurer has nothing to do but painfully retrace his steps and try again in a new direction, as likely as not with the same result. In such a place the rider dismounts and leads his horse, the latter climbing with cat-like agility up seemingly inaccessible heights, scrambling across the steep, sloping shoulders of the bluffs, sliding down the faces of the clay cliffs with all four legs rigid, or dropping from ledge to ledge like a goat, and accepting with unruffled composure an occasional roll from top to bottom. But, in spite of the climbing abilities of the ponies, it is difficult, and at times — for our steeds, at any rate — dangerous work to go through such places, and we only do it when it cannot be avoided. Once I was overtaken by darkness while trying to get through a great tract of very rough land, and, after once or twice nearly breaking my neck, in despair had to give up all attempts to get out, and until daybreak simply staid where I was, in a kind of ledge or pocket on the side of the cliff, luckily sheltered from the wind. It was midsummer and the nights were short, but this particular one seemed quite long enough; and though I was on the move by dawn, it was three hours later before I led the horse, as hungry, numb, and stiff as myself, out on the prairie again.

Occasionally, it is imperatively necessary to cross some of the worst parts of the Bad Lands with a wagon, and such a trip is exhausting and laborious beyond belief. Often the wagon will have to be taken to pieces every few hundred yards in order to get it over a ravine, lower it into a valley, or drag it up a cliff. One outfit, that a year ago tried to take a short cut through some of the Bad Lands of the Powder River, made just four miles in three days, and then had to come back to their starting-point after all. But with only saddle-horses we feel that it must be a very extraordinary country indeed if, in case of necessity, we cannot go through it.

The long forenoon's work, with its attendant mishaps to man and beast, being over, the men who have been out among the horses and cattle come riding in, to be joined by their fellows — if any there be — who have been hunting, or haying, or chopping wood. The midday dinner is variable as to time, for it comes when the men have returned from their work; but, whatever be the hour, it is the most substantial meal of the day, and we feel that we have little fault to find with a table on whose clean cloth are spread platters of smoked elk meat, loaves of good bread, jugs and bowls of milk, saddles of venison or broiled antelope steaks, perhaps roast and fried prairie chickens, with eggs, butter, wild plums, and tea or coffee.

The afternoon's tasks are usually much the same as the morning's, but this time is often spent in doing the odds and ends; as, for instance, it may be devoted to breaking-in a new horse. Large outfits generally hire a bronco-buster to do this; but we ourselves almost always break our own horses, two or three of my men being very good riders, although none of them can claim to be anything out of the common. A first-class flash rider or bronco-buster receives high wages and deserves them, for he follows a most dangerous trade, at which no man can hope to grow old; his work being infinitely harder than that of an Eastern horse-breaker or rough-rider, because he has to do it in such a limited time. A good rider is a good rider all the world over; but an Eastern or English horse-breaker and Western bronco-buster have so little in common with each other as regards style or surroundings, and are so totally out of place in doing each other's work, that it is almost impossible to get either to admit that the other has any merits at all as a horseman, for neither could sit in the saddle of the other or could without great difficulty perform his task. The ordinary Eastern seat, which approaches more or less the seat of a cross-country rider or fox-hunter, is nearly as different from the cowboy's seat as from that of a man who rides bareback. The stirrups on a stock saddle are much farther back than they are on an ordinary English one (a difference far more important than the high horn and cantle of the former),

21

and the man stands nearly erect in them, instead of having his legs bent; and he grips with the thighs and not with the knees, throwing his feet well out. Some of the things he teaches his horse would be wholly useless to an Eastern equestrian: for example, one of the first lessons the newly caught animal has to learn is not to "run on a rope"; and he is taught this by being violently snubbed up, probably turning a somersault, the first two or three times that he feels the noose settle round his neck, and makes a mad rush for liberty. The snubbing-post is the usual adjunct in teaching such a lesson; but a skillful man can do without any help and throw a horse clean over by holding the rope tight against the left haunch, at the same time leaning so far back, with the legs straight in front, that the heels dig deep into the ground when the

22

A HARD TRAIL.

strain comes, and the horse, running out with the slack of the rope, is brought up standing, or even turned head over heels by the shock. Cowboys are probably the only men in the world who invariably wear gloves, buckskin gauntlets being preferred, as otherwise the ropes would soon take every particle of skin off their hands.

A bronco-buster has to work by such violent methods in consequence of the short amount of time at his command. Horses are cheap, each outfit has a great many, and the wages for breaking an animal are but five or ten dollars. Three rides, of an hour or two each, on as many consecutive days, are the outside number a bronco-buster deems necessary before turning an animal over as "broken." The average bronco-buster, however, handles horses so very rudely that we prefer, aside from motives of economy, to break our own; and this is always possible, if we take enough time. The best and most quiet horses on the ranch are far from being those broken by the best riders; on the contrary, they are those that have been handled most gently, although firmly, and that have

sires and dams, yet are quite as wild as the antelope on whose domain they have intruded. Ranchmen run in these wild horses whenever possible, and they are but little more difficult to break than the so-called "tame" animals. But the wild stallions are, whenever possible, shot; both because of their propensity for driving off the ranch mares, and because their incurable viciousness makes them always unsafe companions for other horses still more than

IN WITH THE HORSE HERD.

23

had the greatest number of days devoted to their education.

Some horses, of course, are almost incurably vicious, and must be conquered by main force. One pleasing brute on my ranch will at times rush at a man open-mouthed like a wolf, and this is a regular trick of the range-stallions. In a great many—indeed, in most—localities there are wild horses to be found, which, although invariably of domestic descent, being either themselves runaways from some ranch or Indian outfit, or else claiming such for their

for men. A wild stallion fears no beast except the grizzly, and will not always flinch from an encounter with it; yet it is a curious fact that a jack will almost always kill one in a fair fight. The particulars of a fight of this sort were related to me by a cattle man who was engaged in bringing out blooded stock from the East. Among the animals under his charge were two great stallions, one gray and one black, and a fine jackass, not much over half the size of either of the former. The animals were kept in separate pens, but one day both horses got into the same inclosure, next to the jack-pen, and began to fight as only enraged stallions can, striking like boxers with their fore feet, and biting with their teeth. The gray was getting the best of it; but while clinched with his antagonist in one tussle they rolled against the jack-pen, breaking it in. No sooner was the jack at liberty than, with ears laid back and mouth wide open, he made straight for the two horses, who had for the moment separated. The gray turned to meet him, rearing on his hind legs and striking at him with his fore feet; but the jack slipped in, and in a minute grasped his antagonist by the throat with his wide-open jaws, and then held on like a bull-dog, all four feet planted stiffly in the soil. The stallion made tremendous efforts to shake him off: he would try to whirl round and kick him, but for that the jack was too short; then he would rise up, lifting the jack off the ground, and strike at him with his fore feet; but all that he gained by this was to skin his foe's front legs without making him loose his hold. Twice they fell, and twice the stallion rose, by main strength dragging the jack with him; but all in vain. Meanwhile the black horse attacked both the combatants with perfect impartiality, striking and kicking them with his hoofs, while his teeth, as they slipped off the tough hides, met with a snap like that of a bear-trap. Undoubtedly the jack would have killed at least one of the horses had not the men come up, and with no small difficulty separated the maddened brutes.

If not breaking horses, mending saddles, or doing something else of the sort, the cowboys will often while away their leisure moments by practicing with the rope. A man cannot practice too much with this if he wishes to attain even moderate proficiency; and as a matter of fact he soon gets to wish to practice the whole time. A cowboy is always roping something, and it especially delights him to try his skill at game. A friend of mine, a young ranchman in the Judith basin, about three years ago roped a buffalo, and by the exercise of the greatest skill, both on his own part and on his steed's, actually succeeded, by alternate bullying and coaxing, in getting the huge brute almost into camp. I have occasionally known men on fast horses to rope deer, and even antelope, when circumstances all joined to favor them; and last summer one of the cowboys on a ranch about thirty miles off ran into and roped a wounded elk. A forty-foot lariat is the one commonly used, for the ordinary range at which a man can use it is only about twenty-five feet. Few men can throw forty feet; and to do this, taking into account the coil, needs a sixty-foot rope.

When the day's work is over we take supper, and bed-time comes soon afterward, for the men who live on ranches sleep well and soundly. As a rule, the nights are cool and bracing, even in midsummer; except when we occasionally have a spell of burning weather, with a steady, hot wind that blows in our faces like a furnace blast, sending the thermometer far up above a hundred and making us gasp for breath, even at night, in the dry-baked heat of the air. But it is only rarely that we get a few days of this sort; generally, no matter how unbearable the heat of the day has been, we can at least sleep pleasantly at night.

A ranchman's work is, of course, free from much of the sameness attendant upon that of a mere cowboy. One day he will ride out with his men among the cattle, or after strayed horses; the next he may hunt, so as to keep the ranch in meat; then he can make the tour of his outlying camps; or, again, may join one of the round-ups for a week or two, perhaps keeping with it the entire time it is working. On occasions he will have a good deal of spare time on his hands, which, if he chooses, he can spend in reading or writing. If he cares for books, there will be many a worn volume in the primitive little sitting-room, with its log walls and huge fireplace; but after a hard day's work a man will not read much, but will rock to and fro in the flickering firelight, talking sleepily over his success in the day's chase and the difficulty he has had with the cattle; or else may simply lie stretched at full length on the elk-hides and wolf-skins in front of the hearthstone, listening in drowsy silence to the roar and crackle of the blazing logs and to the moaning of the wind outside.

In the sharp fall weather the riding is delicious all day long; but even in the late spring, and all through the summer, we try, if we can, to do our work before the heat of the day, and if going on a long ride, whether to hunt or for other purposes, leave the ranch house by dawn. The early rides in the spring mornings have a charm all their own, for they are taken when, for the one and only time during the year, the same brown landscape of these high plains turns to a vivid green, as the new grass sprouts and the trees and bushes thrust forth the young leaves; and at dawn, with the dew glittering everywhere, all things show at their best and freshest. The flowers are out and a man may gallop for miles at a stretch with his horse's hoofs sinking at every stride into the carpet of prairie roses, whose short stalks lift the beautiful blossoms but a few inches from the ground. Even in the waste places the cactuses are blooming; and one kind in particu-

24

lar, a dwarfish, globular plant, with its mass of splendid crimson flowers glows against the sides of the gray buttes like a splash of flame.

The ravines, winding about and splitting

out farther to the flat prairie land on the divide. Here, in places, the level, grassy plains are strewn with mounds and hillocks of red or gray scoria, that stand singly or clustered into little groups, their tops crested, or their

A BUCKING BRONCO.

into a labyrinth of coulées, with chains of rounded hills to separate them, have groves of trees in their bottoms, over the sides of the water-courses. In these are found the black-tail deer, and his cousin, the whitetail, too, with his flaunting flag; but in the spring-time, when we are after antelope only, we must go

sides covered, by queer, detached masses of volcanic rock, wrought into strange shapes by the dead forces whose blind, hidden strength long ago called them into being. The road our wagons take, when the water is too high for us to come down the river bottom, stretches far ahead — two dark, straight, parallel furrows which merge into one in the distance. Quaint little horned frogs crawl sluggishly along in the wheel tracks, and the sickle-billed curlews run over the ground or soar above and around the horsemen, uttering their mournful, never-ceasing clamor. The grass-land stretches out in the sunlight like a sea, every wind bending the blades into a ripple, and flecking the prairie with shifting patches of a different green from that around, exactly as the touch of a light squall or wind-gust will fleck the smooth surface of the ocean. Our Western plains differ widely in detail from those of Asia; yet they always call to mind

. . . . The Scythian
On the wide steppe.

In the spring mornings the rider on the plains will hear bird songs unknown in the East. The Missouri sky-lark sings while soaring above the great plateaus so high in the air that it is impossible to see the bird; and this habit of singing while soaring it shares with some sparrow-like birds that are often found in company with it. The white-shouldered lark-bunting, in its livery of black, has rich, full notes, and as it sings on the wing it reminds one of the bobolink; and the sweet-voiced lark-finch also utters its song in the air. These birds, and most of the sparrows of the plains, are characteristic of this region.

But many of our birds, especially those found in the wooded river bottoms, answer to those of the East; only almost each one has some marked point of difference from its Eastern representative. The bluebird out West is very much of a blue bird indeed, for it has no "earth tinge" on its breast at all; while the indigo-bird, on the contrary, has gained the ruddy markings that the other has lost. The flicker has the shafts of its wing and tail quills colored orange instead of yellow. The towhee has lost all title to its name, for its only cry is a mew like that of a cat-bird; while, most wonderful of all, the meadow-lark has found a rich, strong voice, and is one of the sweetest and most incessant singers we have.

Throughout June the thickets and groves about the ranch house are loud with bird music from before dawn till long after sunrise. The thrashers have sung all the night through from among the thorn-bushes if there has been a moon, or even if there has been bright starlight; and before the first glimmer of gray the bell-like, silvery songs of the shy woodland thrushes chime in; while meadow-lark, robin, bluebird, and song sparrow, together with many rarer singers, like the grosbeak, join in swelling the chorus. There are some would-be singers whose intention is better than their execution. Blackbirds of several kinds are plenty round the house and stables, walking about with a knowing air, like so many dwarf crows; and now and then a flock of yellow-heads will mix for a few days with their purple or rusty-colored brethren. The males of these yellow-headed grakles are really handsome, their orange and yellow heads contrasting finely with the black of the rest of their plumage; but their voices are discordant to a degree. When a flock has done feeding it will often light in straggling order among the trees in front of the veranda, and then the males will begin to sing, or rather to utter the most extraordinary collection of broken sounds — creakings, gurglings, hisses, twitters, and every now and then a liquid note or two. It is like an accentuated representation of the noise made by a flock of common blackbirds. At nightfall the poor-wills begin to utter their boding call from the wooded ravines back in the hills; not "whip-poor-will," as in the East, but with two syllables only. They often come round the ranch house. Late one evening I had been sitting motionless on the veranda, looking out across the water and watching the green and brown of the hill-tops change to purple and umber and then fade off into shadowy gray as the somber darkness deepened. Suddenly a poor-will lit on the floor beside me and stayed some little time; now and then uttering its mournful cries, then ceasing for a few moments as it flitted round after insects, and again returning to the same place to begin anew. The little owls, too, call to each other with tremulous, quavering voices throughout the livelong night, as they sit in the creaking trees that overhang the roof. Now and then we hear the wilder voices of the wilderness, from animals that in the hours of darkness do not fear the neighborhood of man: the coyotes wail like dismal ventriloquists, or the silence may be broken by the strident challenge of a lynx, or by the snorting and stamping of a deer that has come to the edge of the open.

In the hot noontide hours of midsummer the broad ranch veranda, always in the shade, is almost the only spot where a man can be comfortable; but here he can sit for hours at a time, leaning back in his rocking-chair as he reads or smokes, or with half-closed, dreamy eyes gazes across the shallow, nearly dry river-bed to the wooded bottoms opposite, and to the plateaus lying back of them. Against the sheer white faces of the cliffs, that come down without a break, the dark green tree-tops stand out in bold relief. In the hot, lifeless air all objects that are not near by seem to sway and waver. There are few sounds to break the stillness. From the upper branches of the cottonwood trees overhead, whose shimmering, tremulous leaves are hardly ever quiet, but if the wind stirs at all, rustle and quaver and sigh all day long, comes every now and then the soft, melancholy cooing of the mourning dove, whose voice always seems far away and expresses more than any other sound in

toss it up with their horns. At times the horses, too, will come down to drink, and to splash and roll in the water.

The prairie-dogs alone are not daunted by the heat, but sit at the mouths of their burrows with their usual pert curiosity. They are both-

CRUISING FOR STOCK.

nature the sadness of gentle, hopeless, never-ending grief. The other birds are still; and very few animals move about. Now and then the black shadow of a wheeling vulture falls on the sun-scorched ground. The cattle, that have strung down in long files from the hills, lie quietly on the sand-bars, except that some of the bulls keep traveling up and down, bellowing and routing or giving vent to long, surly grumblings as they paw the sand and

ersome little fellows, and most prolific, increasing in spite of the perpetual war made on them by every carnivorous bird and beast. One of their worst foes is the black-footed ferret, a handsome, rather rare animal, somewhat like a mink, with a yellow-brown body and dark feet and mask. It is a most bloodthirsty little brute, feeding on all small animals and ground birds. It will readily master a jack-rabbit, will kill very young fawns if it finds them in the mother's absence, and work extraordinary havoc in a dog town, as it can follow the wretched little beasts down into the burrows. In one instance, I knew of a black-footed ferret making a succession of inroads on a ranchman's poultry, killing and carrying off most of them before it was trapped. Coyotes, foxes, swifts, badgers, and skunks also like to lurk about the dog towns. Of the skunks, by the way, we had last year altogether too much; there was a perfect plague of them all along the river, and they took to trying to get into the huts, with the stupid pertinacity of the species. At every ranch house dozens were killed, we ourselves bagging thirty-three, all slain near the house, and one, to our unspeakable sorrow, in it.

In making a journey over ground we know, during the hot weather we often prefer to ride by moonlight. The moon shines very brightly through the dry, clear night air, turning the gray buttes into glimmering silver; and the horses travel far more readily and easily than under the glaring noonday sun. The road between my upper and lower ranch houses is about forty miles long, sometimes following the river-bed, and then again branching off inland, crossing the great plateaus and winding through the ravines of the broken country. It is a five-hours' fair ride; and so, in a hot spell, we like to take it during the cool of the night, starting at sunset. After nightfall the face of the country seems to alter marvelously, and the cool moonlight only intensifies the change. The river gleams like running quicksilver, and the moonbeams play over the grassy stretches of the plateaus and glance off the wind-rippled blades as they would from water. The Bad Lands seem to be stranger and wilder than ever, the silvery rays turning the country into a kind of grim fairy-land. The grotesque, fantastic outlines of the higher cliffs stand out with startling clearness, while the lower buttes have become formless, misshapen masses, and the deep gorges are in black shadow; in the darkness there will be no sound but the rhythmic echo of the hoof-beats of the horses, and the steady, metallic clank of the steel bridle-chains.

But the fall is the time for riding; for in the keen, frosty air neither man nor beast will tire, though out from the dawn until the shadows have again waxed long and the daylight has begun to wane, warning all to push straight for home without drawing rein. Then deer-saddles and elk-haunches hang from the trees near the house; and one can have good sport right on the sand of the river-bed, for we always keep shot-gun or rifle at hand, to be ready for any prairie chickens, or for such of the passing water-fowl as light in the river near us. Occasionally we take a shot at a flock of waders, among which the pretty avocets are the most striking in looks and manners. Prairie fowl are quite plenty all round us, and occasionally small flocks come fairly down into the yard, or perch among the trees near by. At evening they fly down to the river to drink, and as they sit on the sand-bars offer fine marks for the rifles. So do the geese and ducks when they occasionally light on the same places or paddle leisurely down stream in the middle of the river; but to make much of a bag of these we have to use the heavy No. 10, choke-bore shot-gun, while the little 16-bore fowling-piece is much the handiest for prairie fowl. A good many different kinds of water-fowl pass, ranging in size from a teal duck to a Canada goose, and all of them at times help to eke out our bill of fare. Last fall a white-fronted goose lit on the river in front of the ranch house, and three of us, armed with miscellaneous weapons, went out after him; we disabled him, and then after much bad shooting, and more violent running through thick sand and thick underbrush, finally overtook and most foully butchered him. The snow geese and common wild geese are what we usually kill, however.

Sometimes strings of sandhill cranes fly along the river, their guttural clangor being heard very far off. They usually light on a plateau, where sometimes they form rings and go through a series of queer antics, dancing and posturing to each other. They are exceedingly wide-awake birds, and more shy and wary than antelope, so that they are rarely shot; yet once I succeeded in stalking up to a group in the early morning, and firing into them rather at random, my bullet killed a full-grown female. Its breast, when roasted, proved to be very good eating.

Sometimes we vary our diet with fish — wall-eyed pike, ugly, slimy catfish, and other uncouth finny things, looking very fit denizens of the mud-choked water; but they are good eating withal, in spite of their uncanny appearance. We usually catch them with set lines, left out overnight in the deeper pools.

The cattle are fattest and in best condition during the fall, and it is then that the bulk of the beef steers are gathered and shipped — four-year-olds as a rule, though some threes and some fives go along with them. Cattle are a nuisance while hunting on foot, as they either take fright and run off when they see the hunter, scaring all game within sight, or else, what is worse, follow him, blustering and bullying and pretending that they are on the point of charging, but rarely actually doing so. Still, they are occasionally really dangerous,

LINE RIDING IN WINTER.

and it is never entirely safe for a man to be on foot when there is a chance of meeting the droves of long-horned steers. But they will always bluster rather than fight, whether with men or beasts, or with one another. The bulls and some of the steers are forever traveling and challenging each other, never ceasing their hoarse rumbling and moaning and their long-drawn, savage bellowing, tearing up the banks with their horns and sending little spurts of dust above their shoulders with their fore hoofs; yet they do not seem especially fond of real fighting, although, of course, they do occasionally have most desperate and obstinate set-tos with one another. A large bear will make short work of a bull: a few months ago one of the former killed a very big bull near a ranch house a score of miles or so distant, and during one night tore up and devoured a large part of his victim. The ranchman poisoned the carcass and killed the bear.

In the winter there is much less work than at any other season, but what there is involves great hardship and exposure. Many of the

men are discharged after the summer is over, and during much of the cold weather there is little to do except hunt now and then, and in very bitter days lounge about the house. But some of the men are out in the line camps, and the ranchman has occasionally to make the round of these; and besides that, one or more of the cowboys who are at home ought to be out every day when the cattle have become weak, so as to pick up and drive in any beast that will otherwise evidently fail to get through the season — a cow that has had an unusually early calf being particularly apt to need attention. The horses shift for themselves and need no help. Often, in winter, the Indians cut down the cottonwood trees and feed the tops to their ponies; but this is not done to keep them from starving, but only to keep them from wandering off in search of grass. Besides, the ponies are very fond of the bark of the young cottonwood shoots, and it is healthy for them.

The men in the line camps lead a hard life, for they have to be out in every kind of

29

CATTLE DRIFTING BEFORE THE STORM.

weather, and should be especially active and watchful during the storms. The camps are established along some line which it is proposed to make the boundary of the cattle's drift in a given direction. For example, we care very little whether our cattle wander to the Yellowstone; but we strongly object to their drifting east and south-east towards the granger country and the Sioux reservation, especially as when they drift that way they come out on flat, bare plains where there is danger of perishing. Accordingly, the cowmen along the Little Missouri have united in establishing a row of camps to the east of the river, along the line where the broken ground meets the prairie. The camps are usually for two men each, and some fifteen or twenty miles apart; then, in the morning, its two men start out in opposite ways, each riding till he meets his neighbor of the next camp nearest on that side, when he returns. The camp itself is sometimes merely a tent pitched in a sheltered coulée, but ought to be either made of logs or else a dug-out in the ground. A small corral and horse-shed is near by, with enough hay for the ponies, of which each rider has two or three. In riding over the beat each man drives any cattle that have come near it back into the Bad Lands, and if he sees by the hoof-marks that a few have strayed out over the line very recently, he will follow and fetch them home. They must be shoved well back into the Bad Lands before a great storm strikes them; for if they once begin to drift in masses before an icy gale it is impossible for a small number of men to hold them, and the only thing is to let them go, and then to organize an expedition to follow them as soon as possible. Line riding is very cold work, and dangerous too, when the men have to be out in a blinding snow-storm, or in a savage blizzard that takes the spirit in the thermometer far down below zero. In the worst storms it is impossible for any man to be out.

But other kinds of work besides line riding necessitate exposure to bitter weather. Once, while spending a few days over on Beaver Creek hunting up a lost horse, I happened to meet a cowboy who was out on the same errand, and made friends with him. We started home together across the open prairies, but were caught in a very heavy snow-storm almost immediately after leaving the ranch where we had spent the night. We were soon completely turned round, the great soft flakes — for, luckily, it was not cold — almost blinding us, and we had to travel entirely by compass. After feeling our way along for eight or nine hours, we finally got down into the broken country near Sentinel Butte and came across an empty hut, a welcome sight to men as cold, hungry, and tired as we were.   In this hut we passed the night very comfortably, picketing our horses in a sheltered nook near by, with plenty of hay from an old stack. To while away the long evening, I read Hamlet aloud, from a little pocket Shakspere. The cowboy, a Texan,— one of the best riders I have seen, and also a very intelligent as well as a thoroughly good fellow in every way,— was greatly interested in it and commented most shrewdly on the parts he liked, especially Polonius's advice to Laertes, which he translated into more homely language with great relish, and ended with the just criticism that "old Shakspere saveyed human natur' some"— savey being a verb presumably adapted into the limited plains' vocabulary from the French.

Even for those who do not have to look up stray horses, and who are not forced to ride the line day in and day out, there is apt to be some hardship and danger in being abroad during the bitter weather; yet a ride in mid-winter is certainly fascinating.   The great white country wrapped in the powdery snow-drift seems like another land; and the familiar landmarks are so changed that a man must be careful lest he lose his way, for the discomfort of a night in the open during such weather is very great indeed. When the sun is out the glare from the endless white stretches dazzles the eyes; and if the gray snow-clouds hang low and only let a pale, wan light struggle through, the lonely wastes become fairly appalling in their desolation.   For hour after hour a man may go on and see no sign of life except, perhaps, a big white owl sweeping noiselessly by, so that in the dark it looks like a snow-wreath; the cold gradually chilling the rider to the bones, as he draws his fur cap tight over his ears and muffles his face in the huge collar of his wolf-skin coat, and making the shaggy little steed drop head and tail as it picks its way over the frozen soil. There are few moments more pleasant than the home-coming, when, in the gathering darkness, after crossing the last chain of ice-covered buttes, or after coming round the last turn in the wind-swept valley, we see, through the leafless trees, or across the frozen river, the red gleam of the firelight as it shines through the ranch windows and flickers over the trunks of the cottonwoods outside, warming a man's blood by the mere hint of the warmth awaiting him within.

Theodore Roosevelt.

unrelated poem
here

Vol. XXXV   April 1888   No. 6

unrelated poem

here

AN ARIZONA TYPE.

THE ROUND UP

By Theodore Roosevelt
illus by F.R.

DURING the winter-time there is ordinarily but little work done among the cattle. There is some line riding, and a continual lookout is kept for the very weak animals; but most of the stock are left to shift for themselves, undisturbed. Almost every stock-grower's association forbids branding any calves before the spring round-up. If great bands of cattle wander off the range, parties may be fitted out to go after them and bring them back; but this is only done when absolutely necessary, as when the drift of the cattle has been towards an Indian reservation or a settled granger country, for the weather is very severe, and the horses are so poor that their food must be carried along.

The bulk of the work is done during the summer, including the late spring and early fall, and consists mainly in a succession of round-ups, beginning, with us, in May and ending towards the last of October. But a good deal may be done by riding over one's range. Frequently, too, herding will be practiced on a large scale.

More important than herding is "trail" work; cattle, while driven from one range to another, or to a shipping point for beef, being said to be "on the trail." For years, the over-supply from the vast breeding ranches to the south, especially in Texas, has been driven northward in large herds, either to the shipping towns along the great railroads, or else to the fattening ranges of the North-west; it having been found, so far, that while the calf crop is larger in the South, beeves become much heavier in the North. Such cattle, for the most part, went along tolerably well-marked routes or trails, which became for the time

being of great importance, flourishing — and
extremely lawless — towns growing up along
them; but with the growth of the railroad
system, and above all with the filling-up of
the northern ranges, these trails have steadily
become of less and less consequence, though
many herds still travel them on their way to
the already crowded ranges of western Dakota and Montana, or to the Canadian regions beyond. The trail work is something
by itself. The herds may be on the trail several months, averaging fifteen miles or less a
a day. The cowboys accompanying each have
to undergo much hard toil, of a peculiarly
same and wearisome kind, on account of the
extreme slowness with which everything must
be done, as trail cattle should never be hur-
ried. The foreman of a trail outfit must be
not only a veteran cowhand, but also a mira-
cle of patience and resolution.

Round-up work is far less irksome, there
being an immense amount of dash and excitement connected with it; and when once the
cattle are on the range, the important work is
done during the round-up. On cow ranches,
or wherever there is breeding stock, the spring
round-up is the great event of the season, as
it is then that the bulk of the calves are
branded. It usually lasts six weeks, or thereabouts; but its end by no means implies rest
for the stockman. On the contrary, as soon
as it is over, wagons are sent to work out-of-
the-way parts of the country that have been
passed over, but where cattle are supposed to
have drifted; and by the time these have
come back the first beef round-up has begun,
and thereafter beeves are steadily gathered
and shipped, at least from among the larger
herds, until cold weather sets in; and in the
fall there is another round-up, to brand the late
calves and see that the stock is got back on
the range. As all of these round-ups are of one
character, a description of the most important,
taking place in the spring, will be enough.

In April we begin to get up the horses.
Throughout the winter very few have been
kept for use, as they are then poor and weak,
and must be given grain and hay if they are
to be worked. The men in the line camps
need two or three apiece, and each man at
the home ranch has a couple more; but the
rest are left out to shift for themselves, which
the tough, hardy little fellows are well able to
do. Ponies can pick up a living where cattle
die; though the scanty feed, which they may
have to uncover by pawing off the snow, and
the bitter weather often make them look very
gaunt by spring-time. But the first warm
rains bring up the green grass, and then all
the live-stock gain flesh with wonderful rapidity. When the spring round-up begins the

horses should be as fat and sleek as possible.
After running all winter free, even the most
sober pony is apt to betray an inclination to
buck; and, if possible, we like to ride every animal once or twice before we begin to do real
work with him. Animals that have escaped for
any length of time are almost as bad to handle as if they had never been broken. One
of the two horses mentioned in a preceding
article as having been gone eighteen months
has, since his return, been suggestively dubbed
" Dynamite Jimmy," on account of the incessant and eruptive energy with which he bucks.
Many of our horses, by the way, are thus
named from some feat or peculiarity. Wire
Fence, when being broken, ran into one of the
abominations after which he is now called;
Hackamore once got away and remained out
for three weeks with a hackamore, or breaking-
halter, on him; Macaulay contracted the habit
of regularly getting rid of the huge Scotchman
to whom he was intrusted; Bulberry Johnny
spent the hour or two after he was first mounted
in a large patch of thorny bulberry bushes,
his distracted rider unable to get him to do
anything but move round sidewise in a circle; Fall Back would never get to the front;
Water Skip always jumps mud-puddles; and
there are a dozen others with names as purely
descriptive.

The stock-growers of Montana, of the western part of Dakota, and even of portions of
extreme northern Wyoming,— that is, of all the
grazing lands lying in the basin of the Upper
Missouri,— have united, and formed themselves into the great Montana Stock-growers'
Association. Among the countless benefits
they have derived from this course, not the
least has been the way in which the various
round-ups work in with and supplement one
another. At the spring meeting of the association, the entire territory mentioned above,
including perhaps a hundred thousand square
miles, is mapped out into round-up districts,
which generally are changed but slightly from
year to year, and the times and places for the
round-ups to begin refixed so that those of
adjacent districts may be run with a view to
the best interests of all. Thus the stockmen
along the Yellowstone have one round-up;
we along the Little Missouri have another;
and the country lying between, through which
the Big Beaver flows, is almost equally important to both. Accordingly, one spring,
the Little Missouri round-up, beginning May
25 and working down-stream, was timed so
as to reach the mouth of the Big Beaver
about June 1, the Yellowstone round-up beginning at that date and place. Both then
worked up the Beaver together to its head,
when the Yellowstone men turned to the west

33

and we bent back to our own river; thus the bulk of the strayed cattle of each were brought back to their respective ranges. Our own round-up district covers the Big and Little Beaver creeks, which rise near each other, but empty into the Little Missouri nearly a hundred and fifty miles apart, and so much of the latter river as lies between their mouths.

The captain or foreman of the round-up, upon whom very much of its efficiency and success depends, is chosen beforehand. He is, of course, an expert cowman, thoroughly acquainted with the country; and he must also be able to command and to keep control of the wild rough-riders he has under him — a feat needing both tact and firmness.

At the appointed day all meet at the place from which the round-up is to start. Each ranch, of course, has most work to be done in its own round-up district, but it is also necessary to have representatives in all those surrounding it. A large outfit may employ a dozen cowboys, or over, in the home district, and yet have nearly as many more representing its interest in the various ones adjoining. Smaller outfits generally club together to run a wagon and send outside representatives, or else go along with their stronger neighbors, they paying part of the expenses. A large outfit, with a herd of twenty thousand cattle or more, can, if necessary, run a round-up entirely by itself, and is able to act independently of outside help; it is therefore at a great advantage compared with those that can take no step effectively without their neighbors' consent and assistance.

If the starting-point is some distance off, it may be necessary to leave home three or four days in advance. Before this we have got everything in readiness; have overhauled the wagons, shod any horse whose fore feet are tender, — as a rule, all our ponies go barefooted, — and left things in order at the ranch. Our outfit may be taken as a sample of every one else's. We have a stout four-horse wagon to carry the bedding and the food; in its rear a mess-chest is rigged to hold the knives, forks, cans, etc. All our four team-horses are strong, willing animals, though of no great size, being originally just "broncos," or unbroken native horses, like the others. The teamster is also cook: a man who is a really first-rate hand at both driving and cooking — and our present teamster is both — can always command his price. Besides our own men, some cowboys from neighboring ranches and two or three representatives from other round-up districts are always along, and we generally have at least a dozen "riders," as they are termed, — that is, cowboys, or "cow-

puncher," who do the actual cattle-work, — with the wagon. Each of these has a string of eight or ten ponies; and to take charge of the saddle-band, thus consisting of a hundred odd head, there are two herders, always known as "horse-wranglers" — one for the day and one for the night. Occasionally there will be two wagons, one to carry the bedding and one the food, known, respectively, as the bed and the mess wagon; but this is not usual.

While traveling to the meeting-point the pace is always slow, as it is an object to bring the horses on the ground as fresh as possible. Accordingly, we keep at a walk almost all day, and the riders, having nothing else to do, assist the wranglers in driving the saddle-band, three or four going in front, and others on the side, so that the horses shall keep on a walk. There is always some trouble with the animals at the starting out, as they are very fresh and are restive under the saddle. The herd is likely to stampede, and any beast that is frisky or vicious is sure to show its worst side. To do really effective cow-work a pony should be well broken; but many even of the old ones have vicious traits, and almost every man will have in his string one or two young horses, or broncos, hardly broken at all. In consequence, very many of my horses have to this day traits not calculated to set a timid or a clumsy rider at his ease. One or two run away and cannot be held by even the strongest bit; others can hardly be bridled or saddled until they have been thrown; two or three have a tendency to fall over backward; and half of them buck more or less, some so hard that only an expert can sit them.

In riding these wild, vicious horses, and in careering over such very bad ground, especially at night, accidents are always occurring. A man who is merely an ordinary rider is certain to have a pretty hard time. On my first round-up I had a string of nine horses, four of them broncos, only broken to the extent of having each been saddled once or twice. One of them it was an impossibility to bridle or to saddle single-handed; it was very difficult to get on or off him, and he was exceedingly nervous if a man moved his hands or feet; but he had no bad tricks. The second soon became perfectly quiet. The third turned out to be one of the worst buckers on the ranch: once, when he bucked me off, I managed to fall on a stone and broke a rib. The fourth had a still worse habit, for he would balk and then throw himself over backward: once, when I was not quick enough, he caught me and broke something in the point of my shoulder, so that it was some weeks before I could raise the arm freely. My hurts were far from serious, and did not interfere with my riding and working as usual through the round-up; but I was heartily glad when it ended, and ever since have religiously done my best to get none but gentle horses in my own string. However, every one gets falls from or with his horse now and then in the cow country; and even my men, good riders though they are, are sometimes injured. One of them once broke his ankle; another a rib; another was on one occasion stunned, remaining unconscious for some hours; and yet another had certain of his horses buck under him so hard and long as finally to hurt his lungs and make him cough blood. Fatal accidents occur annually in almost every district, especially if there is much work to be done among stampeded cattle at night; but on my own ranch none of my men have ever been seriously hurt, though on one occasion a cowboy from another ranch, who was with my wagon, was killed, his horse falling and pitching him heavily on his head.

For bedding, each man has two or three pairs of blankets, and a tarpaulin or small wagon-sheet. Usually, two or three sleep together. Even in June the nights are generally cool and pleasant, and it is chilly in the early mornings; although this is not always so, and when the weather stays hot and mosquitoes are plenty, the hours of darkness, even in mid-summer, seem painfully long. In the Bad Lands proper we are not often bothered very seriously by these winged pests; but in the low bottoms of the Big Missouri, and beside many of the reedy ponds and great sloughs out on the prairie, they are a perfect scourge. During the very hot nights, when they are especially active, the bed-clothes make a man feel absolutely smothered, and yet his only chance for sleep is to wrap himself tightly up, head and all; and even then some of the pests will usually force their way in. At sunset I have seen the mosquitoes rise up from the land like a dense cloud, to make the hot, stifling night one long torture; the horses would neither lie down nor graze, traveling restlessly to and fro till daybreak, their bodies streaked and bloody, and the insects settling on them so as to make them all one color, a uniform gray; while the men, after a few hours' tossing about in the vain attempt to sleep, rose, built a little fire of damp sage brush, and thus endured the misery as best they could until it was light enough to work.

But if the weather is fine, a man will never sleep better nor more pleasantly than in the open air after a hard day's work on the round-up; nor will an ordinary shower or gust of wind disturb him in the least, for he simply draws the tarpaulin over his head and goes on sleeping. But now and then we have a wind-storm that might better be called a whirlwind and has to be met very differently; and two or three days or nights of rain insure the wetting of the blankets, and therefore shivering discomfort on the part of the would-be sleeper. For two or three hours all goes well; and it is rather soothing to listen to the steady patter of the great raindrops on the canvas. But then it will be found that a corner has been left open through which the water can get in, or else the tarpaulin will begin to leak somewhere; or perhaps the water will have collected in a hollow underneath and have begun to soak through. Soon a little stream trickles in, and every effort to remedy matters merely results in a change for the worse. To move out of the way insures getting wet in a fresh spot; and the best course is to lie still and accept the evils that have come with what fortitude one can. Even thus, the first night a man can sleep pretty well; but if the rain continues, the second night, when the blankets are already damp, and when the water comes through more easily, is apt to be most unpleasant.

Of course, a man can take little spare clothing on a round-up; at the very outside two or three clean handkerchiefs, a pair of socks, a change of underclothes, and the most primitive kind of washing apparatus, all wrapped up in a stout jacket which is to be worn when night-herding. The inevitable "slicker," or oil-skin coat, which gives complete protection from the wet, is always carried behind the saddle.

At the meeting-place there is usually a delay of a day or two to let every one come in; and the plain on which the encampment is made becomes a scene of great bustle and turmoil. The heavy four-horse wagons jolt in from different quarters, the horse-wranglers rushing madly to and fro in the endeavor to keep the different saddle-bands from mingling, while the "riders," or cowboys, with each wagon jog along in a body. The representatives from outside districts ride in singly or by twos and threes, every man driving before him his own horses, one of them loaded with his bedding. Each wagon wheels out of the way into some camping-place not too near the others, the bedding is tossed out on the ground, and then every one is left to do what he wishes, while the different wagon bosses, or foremen, seek out the captain of the round-up to learn what his plans are.

There is a good deal of rough but effective discipline and method in the way in which a round-up is carried on. The captain of the whole has as lieutenants the various wagon foremen, and in making demands for men to do some special service he will usually merely

THE ROUND-UP.

36

designate some foreman to take charge of the work and let him parcel it out among his men to suit himself. The captain of the round-up or the foreman of a wagon may himself be a ranchman; if such is not the case, and the ranchman nevertheless comes along, he works and fares precisely as do the other cowboys.

While the head men are gathered in a little knot, planning out the work, the others are dispersed over the plain in every direction, racing, breaking rough horses, or simply larking with one another. If a man has an especially bad horse, he usually takes such an opportunity, when he has plenty of time, to ride him; and while saddling he is surrounded by a crowd of most unsympathetic associates who greet with uproarious mirth any misadventure. A

may reserve all his energies for the rider. In the last case, the man, keeping tight hold with his left hand of the cheek-strap, so as to prevent the horse from getting his head down until he is fairly seated, swings himself quickly into the saddle. Up rises the bronco's back into an arch; his head, the ears laid straight back, goes down between his fore feet, and, squealing savagely, he makes a succession of rapid, stiff-legged, jarring bounds. Sometimes he is a "plunging" bucker, who runs forward all the time while bucking; or he may buck steadily in one place, or "sunfish,"—that is, bring first one shoulder down almost to the ground and then the other,—or else he may change ends while in the air. A first-class rider will sit throughout it all without moving from the sad-

THE ROPE CORRAL.

man on a bucking horse is always considered fair game, every squeal and jump of the bronco being hailed with cheers of delighted irony for the rider and shouts to "stay with him." The antics of a vicious bronco show infinite variety of detail, but are all modeled on one general plan. When the rope settles round his neck the fight begins, and it is only after much plunging and snorting that a twist is taken over his nose, or else a hackamore — a species of severe halter, usually made of plaited hair — slipped on his head. While being bridled he strikes viciously with his fore feet, and perhaps has to be blindfolded or thrown down; and to get the saddle on him is quite as difficult. When saddled, he may get rid of his exuberant spirits by bucking under the saddle, or

dle, quirting * his horse all the time, though his hat may be jarred off his head and his revolver out of its sheath. After a few jumps, however, the average man grasps hold of the horn of the saddle — the delighted onlookers meanwhile earnestly advising him not to "go to leather"— and is contented to get through the affair in any shape provided he can escape without being thrown off. An accident is of necessity borne with a broad grin, as any attempt to resent the raillery of the bystanders — which is perfectly good-humored — would be apt to result disastrously. Cowboys are certainly extremely good riders. As a class they

* Quirt is the name of the short flexible riding-whip used throughout cowboy land. The term is a Spanish one.

37

have no superiors. Of course, they would at first be at a disadvantage in steeple-chasing or fox-hunting, but their average of horsemanship is without doubt higher than that of the men who take part in these latter amusements. A cowboy would learn to ride across country in a quarter of the time it would take a cross-country rider to learn to handle a vicious bronco or to do good cow-work round and in a herd.

On such a day, when there is no regular work, there will often also be horse-races, as each outfit is pretty sure to have some running pony which it believes can outpace any other. These contests are always short-distance dashes, for but a few hundred yards. Horse-racing is a mania with most plainsmen, white or red. A man with a good racing pony will travel all about with it, often winning large sums, visiting alike cow ranches, frontier towns, and Indian encampments. Sometimes the race is "pony against pony," the victor taking both steeds. In racing the men ride bareback, as there are hardly any light saddles in the cow country. There will be intense excitement and very heavy betting over a race between two well-known horses, together with a good chance of blood being shed in the attendant quarrels. Indians and whites often race against each other as well as among themselves. I have seen several such contests, and in every case but one the white man happened to win. A race is usually run between two thick rows of spectators, on foot and on horseback, and as the racers pass, these rows close in behind them, every man yelling and shouting with all the strength of his lungs, and all waving their hats and cloaks to encourage the contestants, or firing off their revolvers and saddle guns. The little horses are fairly maddened, as is natural enough, and run as if they were crazy: were the distances longer, some would be sure to drop in their tracks.

Besides the horse-races, which are, of course, the main attraction, the men at a round-up will often get up wrestling matches or footraces. In fact, every one feels that he is off for a holiday; for after the monotony of a long winter, the cowboys look forward eagerly to the round-up, where the work is hard, it is true, but exciting and varied, and treated a good deal as a frolic. There is no eight-hour law in cowboy land: during round-up time we often count ourselves lucky if we get off with much less than sixteen hours; but the work is done in the saddle, and the men are spurred on all the time by the desire to outdo one another in feats of daring and skillful horsemanship. There is very little quarreling or fighting; and though the fun often takes the form of rather rough horse-play, yet the practice

of carrying dangerous weapons makes cowboys show far more rough courtesy to each other and far less rudeness to strangers than is the case among, for instance, Eastern miners, or even lumbermen. When a quarrel may very probably result fatally, a man thinks twice before going into it: warlike people or classes always treat one another with a certain amount of consideration and politeness. The moral tone of a cow-camp, indeed, is rather high than otherwise. Meanness, cowardice, and dishonesty are not tolerated. There is a high regard for truthfulness and keeping one's word, intense contempt for any kind of hypocrisy, and a hearty dislike for a man who shirks his work. Many of the men gamble and drink, but many do neither; and the conversation is not worse than in most bodies composed wholly of male human beings. A cowboy will not submit tamely to an insult, and is very ready to avenge his own wrongs; nor has he an overwrought fear of shedding blood. He possesses, in fact, few of the emasculated, milk-and-water moralities admired by the pseudo-philanthropists; but he does possess, to a very high degree, the stern, manly qualities that are so valuable to a nation.

The method of work is simple. The mess-wagons and loose horses, after breaking camp in the morning, move on in a straight line for some few miles, going into camp again before midday; and the day herd, consisting of all the cattle that have been found far off their range, and which are to be brought back there, and of any others that it is necessary to gather, follows on afterwards. Meanwhile the cowboys scatter out and drive in all the cattle from the country round about, going perhaps ten or fifteen miles back from the line of march, and meeting at the place where camp has already been pitched. The wagons always keep some little distance from one another, and the saddle-bands do the same, so that the horses may not get mixed. It is rather picturesque to see the four-horse teams filing down at a trot through a pass among the buttes — the saddle-bands being driven along at a smart pace to one side or behind, the teamsters cracking their whips, and the horse-wranglers calling and shouting as they ride rapidly from side to side behind the horses, urging on the stragglers by dexterous touches with the knotted ends of their long lariats that are left trailing from the saddle. The country driven over is very rough, and it is often necessary to double up teams and put on eight horses to each wagon in going up an unusually steep pitch, or hauling through a deep mud-hole, or over a river crossing where there is quicksand.

The speed and thoroughness with which a

DRIVING TO THE ROUND-UP.

country can be worked depends, of course, very largely upon the number of riders. Ours is probably about an average round-up as regards size. The last spring I was out, there were half a dozen wagons along; the saddle-bands numbered about a hundred each; and the morning we started, sixty men in the saddle splashed across the shallow ford of the river that divided the plain where we had camped from the valley of the long winding creek up which we were first to work.

In the morning, the cook is preparing breakfast long before the first glimmer of dawn. As soon as it is ready, probably about 3 o'clock, he utters a long-drawn shout, and all the sleepers feel it is time to be up on the instant, for they know there can be no such thing as delay on the round-up, under penalty of being set afoot. Accordingly, they bundle out, rubbing their eyes and yawning, draw on their boots and trousers,—if they have taken the latter off,—roll up and cord their bedding, and usually without any attempt at washing crowd over to the little smoldering fire, which is placed in a hole dug in the ground, so that there may be no risk of its spreading. The

men are rarely very hungry at breakfast, and it is a meal that has to be eaten in shortest order, so it is perhaps the least important. Each man, as he comes up, grasps a tin cup and plate from the mess-box, pours out his tea or coffee, with sugar, but of course no milk, helps himself to one or two of the biscuits that have been baked in a Dutch oven, and perhaps also to a slice of the fat pork swimming in the grease of the frying-pan, ladles himself out some beans, if there are any, and squats down on the ground to eat his breakfast. The meal is not an elaborate one; nevertheless a man will have to hurry if he wishes to eat it before hearing the foreman sing out, " Come, boys, catch your horses"; when he must drop everything and run out to the wagon with his lariat. The night wrangler is now bringing in the saddle-band, which he has been up all night guarding. A rope corral is rigged up by stretching a rope from each wheel of one side of the wagon, making a V-shaped space, into which the saddle-horses are driven. Certain men stand around to keep them inside, while the others catch the horses: many outfits have one man to do all the roping. As soon as each

39

has caught his horse — usually a strong, tough animal, the small, quick ponies being reserved for the work round the herd in the afternoon — the band, now in charge of the day wrangler, is turned loose, and every one saddles up as fast as possible. It still lacks some time of being sunrise, and the air has in it the peculiar chill of the early morning. When all are saddled, many of the horses bucking and dancing about, the riders from the different wagons all assemble at the one where the captain is sitting, already mounted. He waits a very short time — for laggards receive but scant mercy — before announcing the proposed camping-place and parceling out the work among those present. If, as is usually the case, the line of march is along a river or creek, he appoints some man to take a dozen others and drive down (or up) it ahead of the day herd, so that the latter will not have to travel through other cattle; the day herd

Meanwhile the two bands, a score of riders in each, separate and make their way in opposite directions. The leader of each tries to get such a "scatter" on his men that they will cover completely all the land gone over. This morning work is called circle riding, and is peculiarly hard in the Bad Lands on account of the remarkably broken, rugged nature of the country. The men come in on lines that tend to a common center — as if the sticks of a fan were curved. As the band goes out, the leader from time to time detaches one or two men to ride down through certain sections of the country, making the shorter, or what are called inside, circles, while he keeps on; and finally, retaining as companions the two or three whose horses are toughest, makes the longest or outside circle himself, going clear back to the divide, or whatever the point may be that marks the limit of the round-up work, and then turning and working straight to the meet-

SADDLING FRESH HORSES.

itself being driven and guarded by a dozen men detached for that purpose. The rest of the riders are divided into two bands, placed under men who know the country, and start out, one on each side, to bring in every head for fifteen miles back. The captain then himself rides down to the new camping-place, so as to be there as soon as any cattle are brought in.

ing-place. Each man, of course, brings in every head of cattle he can see.

These long, swift rides in the glorious spring mornings are not soon to be forgotten. The sweet, fresh air, with a touch of sharpness thus early in the day, and the rapid motion of the fiery little horse combine to make a man's blood thrill and leap with sheer buoyant light-heartedness and eager, exultant pleasure in the boldness and freedom of the life he is leading. As we climb the steep sides of the first range of buttes, wisps of wavering mist still cling in the hollows of the valley; when we come out on the top of the first great plateau, the sun flames up over its edge, and in the level, red beams the galloping horsemen throw long fantastic shadows. Black care rarely sits behind a rider whose pace is fast enough; at any rate, not when he first feels the horse move under him.

Sometimes we trot or pace, and again we lope or gallop; the few who are to take the outside circle must needs ride both hard and fast. Although only grass-fed, the horses are tough and wiry; and, moreover, are each used but once in four days, or thereabouts, so they

wet weather the Bad Lands are absolutely impassable; but if the ground is not slippery, it is a remarkable place that can shake the matter-of-course confidence felt by the rider in the capacity of his steed to go anywhere.

When the men on the outside circle have reached the bound set them,— whether it is a low divide, a group of jagged hills, the edge of the rolling, limitless prairie, or the long, waste reaches of alkali and sage brush,— they turn their horses' heads and begin to work down the branches of the creeks, one or two riding down the bottom, while the others keep off to the right and the left, a little ahead and fairly high up on the side hills, so as to command as much of a view as possible. On the level or rolling prairies the cattle can be seen a long way off, and it is an easy matter to gather and to drive them; but in the Bad Lands

ROPED!

stand the work well. The course out lies across great grassy plateaus, along knife-like ridge crests, among winding valleys and ravines, and over acres of barren, sun-scorched buttes, that look grimly grotesque and forbidding, while in the Bad Lands the riders unhesitatingly go down and over places where it seems impossible that a horse should even stand. The line of horsemen will quarter down the side of a butte, where every pony has to drop from ledge to ledge like a goat, and will go over the shoulder of a soapstone cliff, when wet and slippery, with a series of plunges and scrambles which if unsuccessful would land horses and riders in the bottom of the cañon-like washout below. In descending a clay butte after a rain, the pony will put all four feet together and slide down to the bottom almost or quite on his haunches. In very

every little pocket, basin, and coulée has to be searched, every gorge or ravine entered, and the dense patches of brushwood and spindling, wind-beaten trees closely examined. All the cattle are carried on ahead down the creek; and it is curious to watch the different behavior of the different breeds. A cowboy riding off to one side of the creek, and seeing a number of long-horned Texans grazing in the branches of a set of coulées, has merely to ride across the upper ends of these, uttering the drawn-out "ei-koh-h-h," so familiar to the cattle-men, and the long-horns will stop grazing, stare fixedly at him, and then, wheeling, strike off down the coulées at a trot, tails in air, to be carried along by the center riders when they reach the main creek into which the coulées lead. Our own range cattle are not so wild, but nevertheless are easy to drive; while Eastern-raised beasts have little fear of a horseman, and merely stare stupidly

41

CUTTING OUT A STEER.

at him until he rides directly towards them. Every little bunch of stock is thus collected, and all are driven along together. At the place where some large fork joins the main creek another band may be met, driven by some of the men who have left earlier in the day to take one of the shorter circles; and thus, before coming down to the bottom where the wagons are camped and where the actual "round-up" itself is to take place, this one herd may include a couple of thousand head; or, on the other hand, the longest ride may not result in the finding of a dozen animals. As soon as the riders are in, they disperse to their respective wagons to get dinner and change horses, leaving the cattle to be held by one or two of their number. If only a small number of cattle have been gathered, they will all be run into one herd; if there are many of them, however, the different herds will be held separate.

A plain where a round-up is taking place offers a picturesque sight. I well remember one such. It was on a level bottom in the bend of the river, which here made an almost semi-circular sweep. The bottom was in shape a long oval, hemmed in by an unbroken line of steep bluffs so that it looked like an amphitheater. Across the faces of the dazzling white cliffs there were sharp bands of black and red, drawn by the coal seams and the layers of burned clay: the leaves of the trees and the grass had the vivid green of spring-time. The wagons were camped among the cottonwood trees fringing the river, a thin column of smoke rising up from beside each. The horses were grazing round the outskirts, those of each wagon by themselves and kept from going

BRANDING A HORSE.

too near the others by their watchful guard. In the great circular corral, towards one end, the men were already branding calves, while the whole middle of the bottom was covered with lowing herds of cattle and shouting, galloping cowboys. Apparently there was nothing but dust, noise, and confusion; but in reality the work was proceeding all the while with the utmost rapidity and certainty.

As soon as, or even before, the last circle riders have come in and have snatched a few hasty mouthfuls to serve as their midday meal, we begin to work the herd — or herds, if the one herd would be of too unwieldy size. The animals are held in a compact bunch, most of the riders forming a ring outside, while a couple from each ranch successively look the herds through and cut out those marked with their own brand. It is difficult, in such a mass of moving beasts,— for they do not stay still, but keep weaving in and out among each other,— to find all of one's own animals: a man must have natural gifts, as well as great experience, before he becomes a good brand-reader and is able to really "clean up a herd"— that is, be sure he has left nothing of his own in it.

To do good work in cutting out from a herd, not only should the rider be a good horseman, but he should also have a skillful, thoroughly trained horse. A good cutting pony is not common, and is generally too valuable to be used anywhere but in the herd. Such an one enters thoroughly into the spirit of the thing,

and finds out immediately the animal his master is after; he will then follow it closely of his own accord through every wheel and double, at top speed. When looking through the herd, it is necessary to move slowly; and when any animal is found it is taken to the outskirts at a walk, so as not to alarm the others. Once at the outside, however, the cowboy has to ride like lightning; for as soon as the beast he is after finds itself separated from its companions it endeavors to break back among them, and a young, range-raised steer or heifer runs like a deer. In cutting out a cow and a calf two men have to work together. As the animals of a brand are cut out they are received and held apart by some rider detailed for the purpose, who is said to be " holding the cut."

All this time the men holding the herd have their hands full, for some animal is continually trying to break out, when the nearest man flies at it at once and after a smart chase brings it back to its fellows. As soon as all the cows, calves, and whatever else is being gathered have been cut out, the rest are driven clear off the ground and turned loose, being headed in the direction contrary to that in which we travel the following day. Then the riders surround the next herd, the men holding cuts move them up near it, and the work is begun anew.

If it is necessary to throw an animal, either to examine a brand or for any other reason, half a dozen men will have their ropes down at once; and then it is spur and quirt in

43

the rivalry to see which can outdo the other until the beast is roped and thrown. A first-class hand will, unaided, rope, throw, and tie down a cow or steer in wonderfully short time: one of the favorite tests of competitive skill among the cowboys is the speed with which this feat can be accomplished. Usually, however, one man ropes the animal by the head and another at the same time gets the loop of his lariat over one or both its hind legs, when it is twisted over and stretched out in a second. In following an animal on horseback the man keeps steadily swinging the rope round his head, by a dexterous motion of the wrist only, until he gets a chance to throw it; when on foot, especially if catching horses in a corral, the loop is allowed to drag loosely on the ground. A good roper will hurl out the coil with marvelous accuracy and force; it fairly whistles through the air, and settles round the object with almost infallible certainty. Mexicans make the best ropers; but some Texans are very little behind them. A good horse takes as much interest in the work as does his rider, and the instant the noose settles over the victim wheels and braces himself to meet the shock, standing with his legs firmly planted, the steer or cow being thrown with a jerk. An unskillful rider and an untrained horse will often themselves be thrown when the strain comes.

Sometimes an animal — usually a cow or steer, but, strangely enough, very rarely a bull —will get fighting mad, and turn on the men. If on the drive, such a beast usually is simply dropped out; but if they have time, nothing delights the cowboys more than an encounter of this sort, and the charging brute is roped and tied down in short order. Often such a one will make a very vicious fight, and is most dangerous. Once a fighting cow kept several of us busy for nearly an hour; she gored two ponies, one of them, which was, luckily, hurt but slightly, being my own pet cutting horse. If a steer is hauled out of a mudhole, its first act is usually to charge the rescuer.

As soon as all the brands of cattle are worked, and the animals that are to be driven along have been put in the day herd, attention is turned to the cows and calves, which are already gathered in different bands, consisting each of all the cows of a certain brand and all the calves that are following them. If there is a corral, each band is in turn driven into it; if there is none, a ring of riders does duty in its place. A fire is built, the irons heated, and a dozen men dismount to, as it is called, "wrestle" the calves. The best two ropers go in on their horses to catch the latter; one man keeps tally, a couple put on the brands, and the others seize, throw, and hold the little unfortunates. A first-class roper invariably catches the calf by both hind feet, and then, having taken a twist with his lariat round the horn of the saddle, drags the bawling little creature, extended at full length, up to the fire, where it is held before it can make a struggle. A less skillful roper catches round the neck, and then, if the calf is a large one, the man who seizes it has his hands full, as the bleating, bucking animal develops astonishing strength, cuts the wildest capers, and resists frantically and with all its power. If there are seventy or eighty calves in a corral, the scene is one of the greatest confusion. The ropers, spurring and checking the fierce little horses, drag the calves up so quickly that a dozen men can hardly hold them; the men with the irons, blackened with soot, run to and fro; the calf-wrestlers, grimy with blood, dust, and sweat, work like beavers; while with

BRANDING A CALF.

44

the voice of a stentor the tally-man shouts out the number and sex of each calf. The dust rises in clouds, and the shouts, cheers, curses, and laughter of the men unite with the lowing of the cows and the frantic bleating of the roped calves to make a perfect babel. Now and then an old cow turns vicious and puts every one out of the corral. Or a *maverick* bull,— that is, an unbranded bull,— a yearling or a two-years-old, is caught, thrown, and branded; when he is let up, there is sure to be a fine scatter. Down goes his head, and he bolts at the nearest man, who makes out of the way at top speed, amidst roars of laughter from all of his companions; while the men holding down calves swear savagely as they dodge charging mavericks, trampling horses, and taut lariats with frantic, plunging little beasts at the farther ends.

Every morning certain riders are detached to drive and to guard the day herd, which is most monotonous work, the men being on from 4 in the morning till 8 in the evening, the only rest coming at dinner-time, when they change horses. When the herd has reached the camping-ground there is nothing to do but to loll listlessly over the saddle-bow in the blazing sun, watching the cattle feed and sleep, and seeing that they do not spread out too much. Plodding slowly along on the trail through the columns of dust stirred up by the hoofs is not much better. Cattle travel best and fastest strung out in long lines; the swiftest taking the lead in single file, while the weak and the lazy, the young calves and the poor cows, crowd together in the rear. Two men travel along with the leaders, one on each side, to point them in the right direction; one or two others keep by the flanks, and the rest are in the rear to act as "drag-drivers" and hurry up the phalanx of reluctant weaklings. If the foremost of the string travels too fast, one rider will go along on the trail a few rods ahead, and thus keep them back so that those in the rear will not be left behind.

Generally all this is very tame and irksome; but by fits and starts there will be little flurries of excitement. Two or three of the circle riders may unexpectedly come over a butte near by with a bunch of cattle, which at once start for the day herd, and then there will be a few minutes' furious riding hither and thither to keep them out. Or the cattle may begin to run, and then get "milling"—that is, all crowd together into a mass like a ball, wherein they move round and round, trying to keep their heads towards the center, and refusing to leave it. The only way to start them is to force one's horse in among them and cut out some of their number, which then begin to travel off by themselves, when the others will probably follow. But in spite of occasional incidents of this kind, day-herding has a dreary sameness about it that makes the men dislike and seek to avoid it.

From 8 in the evening till 4 in the morning the day herd becomes a night herd. Each wagon in succession undertakes to guard it for a night, dividing the time into watches of two hours apiece, a couple of riders taking each watch. This is generally chilly and tedious; but at times it is accompanied by intense excitement and danger, when the cattle become stampeded, whether by storm or otherwise. The first and the last watches are those chosen by preference; the others are disagreeable, the men having to turn out cold and sleepy, in the pitchy darkness, the two hours of chilly wakefulness completely breaking the night's rest. The first guards have to bed the cattle down, though the day-herders often do this themselves: it simply consists in hemming them into as small a space as possible, and then riding round them until they lie down and fall asleep. Often, especially at first, this takes some time — the beasts will keep rising and lying down again. When at last most become quiet, some perverse brute of a steer will deliberately hook them all up; they keep moving in and out among one another, and long strings of animals suddenly start out from the herd at a stretching walk, and are turned back by the nearest cowboy only to break forth at a new spot. When finally they have lain down and are chewing their cud or slumbering, the two night guards begin riding round them in opposite ways, often, on very dark nights, calling or singing to them, as the sound of the human voice on such occasions seems to have a tendency to quiet them. In inky black weather, especially when rainy, it is both difficult and unpleasant work; the main trust must be placed in the horse, which, if old at the business, will of its own accord keep pacing steadily round the herd, and head off any animals that, unseen by the rider's eyes in the darkness, are trying to break out. Usually the watch passes off without incident, but on rare occasions the cattle become restless and prone to stampede. Anything may then start them — the plunge of a horse, the sudden approach of a coyote, or the arrival of some outside steers or cows that have smelt them and come up. Every animal in the herd will be on its feet in an instant, as if by an electric shock, and off with a rush, horns and tail up. Then, no matter how rough the ground nor how pitchy black the night, the cowboys must ride for all there is in them and spare neither their own nor their horses' necks. Perhaps their charges break away and are lost altogether; perhaps, by

THE HERD AT NIGHT.

46

desperate galloping, they may head them off, get them running in a circle, and finally stop them. Once stopped, they may break again, and possibly divide up, one cowboy, perhaps, following each band. I have known six such stops and renewed stampedes to take place in one night, the cowboy staying with his ever-diminishing herd of steers until daybreak, when he managed to get them under control again, and, by careful humoring of his jaded, staggering horse, finally brought those that were left back to the camp several miles distant. The riding in these night stampedes is wild and dangerous to a degree, especially if the man gets caught in the rush of the beasts. It also frequently necessitates an immense amount of work in collecting the scattered animals. On one such occasion a small party of us were thirty-six hours in the saddle, dismounting only to change horses or to eat. We were almost worn out at the end of the time; but it must be kept in mind that for a long spell of such work a stock-saddle is far less tiring than the ordinary Eastern or English one, and in every way superior to it.

By very hard riding, such a stampede may

sometimes be prevented. Once we were bringing a thousand head of young cattle down to my lower ranch, and as the river was high were obliged to take the inland trail. The third night we were forced to make a dry camp, the cattle having had no water since the morning. Nevertheless, we got them bedded down without difficulty, and one of the cowboys and myself stood first guard. But very soon after nightfall, when the darkness had become complete, the thirsty brutes of one accord got on their feet and tried to break out. The only salvation was to keep them close together, as, if they once got scattered, we knew they could never be gathered; so I kept on one side, and the cowboy on the other, and never in my life did I ride so hard. In the darkness I could but dimly see the shadowy outlines of the herd, as with whip and spurs I ran the pony along its edge, turning back the beasts at one point barely in time to wheel and keep them in at another. The ground was cut up by numerous little gullies, and each of us got several falls, horses and riders turning complete somersaults. We were dripping with sweat, and our ponies quivering and trembling like quaking aspens, when, after more than an hour of the most violent exertion, we finally got the herd quieted again.

On another occasion while with the round-up we were spared an excessively unpleasant night only because there happened to be two or three great corrals not more than a mile or so away. All day long it had been raining heavily, and we were well drenched; but towards evening it lulled a little, and the day herd, a very large one, of some two thousand head, was gathered on an open bottom. We had turned the horses loose, and in our oil-skin slickers cowered, soaked and comfortless, under the lee of the wagon, to take a meal of damp bread and lukewarm tea, the sizzling embers of the fire having about given up the ghost after a fruitless struggle with the steady downpour. Suddenly the wind began to come in quick, sharp gusts, and soon a regular blizzard was blowing, driving the rain in stinging level sheets before it. Just as we were preparing to turn into bed, with the certainty of a night of more or less chilly misery ahead of us, one of my men, an iron-faced personage, whom no one would ever have dreamed had a weakness for poetry, looked towards the plain where the cattle were, and remarked, " I guess there 's 'racing and chasing on Cannobie Lea' now, sure." Following his gaze, I saw that the cattle had begun to drift before the storm, the night guards being evidently unable to cope with them, while at the other wagons riders were saddling in hot haste and spurring

off to their help through the blinding rain. Some of us at once ran out to our own saddle-band. All of the ponies were standing huddled together, with their heads down and their tails to the wind. They were wild and restive enough usually; but the storm had cowed them, and we were able to catch them without either rope or halter. We made quick work of saddling; and the second each man was ready, away he loped through the dusk, splashing and slipping in the pools of water that studded the muddy plain. Most of the riders were already out when we arrived. The cattle were gathered in a compact, wedge-shaped, or rather fan-shaped mass, with their tails to the wind — that is, towards the thin end of the wedge or fan. In front of this fan-shaped mass of frightened, maddened beasts was a long line of cowboys, each muffled in his slicker and with his broad hat pulled down over his eyes, to shield him from the pelting rain. When the cattle were quiet for a moment every horseman at once turned round with his back to the wind, and the whole line stood as motionless as so many sentries. Then, if the cattle began to spread out and overlap at the ends, or made a rush and broke through at one part of the lines, there would be a change into wild activity. The men, shouting and swaying in their saddles, darted to and fro with reckless speed, utterly heedless of danger — now racing to the threatened point, now checking and wheeling their horses so sharply as to bring them square on their haunches, or even throw them flat down, while the hoofs plowed long furrows in the slippery soil, until, after some minutes of this mad galloping hither and thither, the herd, having drifted a hundred yards or so, would be once more brought up standing. We always had to let them drift a little to prevent their spreading out too much. The din of the thunder was terrific, peal following peal until they mingled in one continuous, rumbling roar; and at every thunder-clap louder than its fellows the cattle would try to break away. Darkness had set in, but each flash of lightning showed us a dense array of tossing horns and staring eyes. It grew always harder to hold in the herd; but the drift took us along to the corrals already spoken of, whose entrances were luckily to windward. As soon as we reached the first we cut off part of the herd, and turned it within; and after again doing this with the second, we were able to put all the remaining animals into the third. The instant the cattle were housed five-sixths of the horsemen started back at full speed for the wagons; the rest of us barely waited to put up the bars and make the corrals secure before galloping after them. We had to ride right in the teeth of the driv-

47

IN A STAMPEDE.

48

ing storm; and once at the wagons we made small delay in crawling in under our blankets, damp though the latter were, for we were ourselves far too wet, stiff, and cold not to hail with grateful welcome any kind of shelter from the wind and the rain.

All animals were benumbed by the violence of this gale of cold rain: a prairie-chicken rose from under my horse's feet so heavily that, thoughtlessly striking at it, I cut it down with my whip; while when a jack rabbit got up ahead of us, it was barely able to limp clumsily out of our way.

But though there is much work and hardship, rough fare, monotony, and exposure connected with the round-up, yet there are few

TRAILING CATTLE.

men who do not look forward to it and back to it with pleasure. The only fault to be found is that the hours of work are so long that one does not usually have enough time to sleep. The food, if rough, is good. The men are good-humored, bold, and thoroughly interested in their business, continually vying with one another in the effort to see which can do the work best. It is superbly health-giving, and is full of excitement and adventure, calling for the exhibition of pluck, self-reliance, hardihood, and dashing horsemanship; and of all forms of physical labor the easiest and pleasantest is to sit in the saddle.

The scenery is often exceedingly striking in character, especially in the Bad Lands, with their queer fantastic formations. Among the most interesting features are the burning mines. These are formed by the coal seams that get on fire. They vary greatly in size. Some send up smoke-columns that are visible miles away, while others are not noticeable a few rods off. The old ones gradually burn away, while new ones unexpectedly break out. Thus, last fall, one suddenly appeared but half a mile from the ranch house. We never knew it was there until one cold moonlight night, when we were riding home, we rounded the corner of a ravine and saw in our path a tall white column of smoke rising from a rift in the snowy crags ahead of us. As the trail was over perfectly familiar ground, we were for a moment almost as startled as if we had seen a ghost.

The burning mines are uncanny places, anyhow. A strong smell of sulphur hangs round them, the heated earth crumbles and cracks, and through the long clefts that form in it we can see the lurid glow of the subterranean fires, with here and there tongues of blue or cherry colored flame dancing up to the surface.

The winters vary greatly in severity with us. During some seasons men can go lightly clad even in January and February, and the cattle hardly suffer at all; during others there will be spells of bitter weather, accompanied by furious blizzards, which render it impossible for days and weeks at a time for men to stir out-of-doors at all, save at the risk of their lives. Then line rider, ranchman, hunter, and teamster alike all have to keep within doors. I have known of several cases of men freezing to death when caught in shelterless places by such a blizzard, a strange fact being that in about half of them the doomed man had evidently gone mad before dying, and had stripped himself of most of his clothes, the body when found being nearly naked. On our ranch we have never had any bad accidents, although every winter some of us get more or less frost-bitten. My last experience in this line was while returning by moonlight

49

from a successful hunt after mountain sheep. The thermometer was 26° below zero, and we had had no food for twelve hours. I got numbed, and before I was aware of it had frozen my face, one foot, both knees, and one hand. Luckily, I reached the ranch before serious damage was done. About once every six or seven years we have a season when these storms follow one another almost without interval throughout the winter months, and then the loss among the stock is frightful. One such winter occurred in 1880–81. This was when there were very few ranchmen in the country. The next severe winter was that of 1886–87, when the rush of incoming herds had overstocked the ranges, and the loss was in consequence fairly appalling.

The snow-fall was unprecedented, both for its depth and for the way it lasted; and it was this, and not the cold, that caused the loss. About the middle of November the storms began. Day after day the snow came down, thawing and then freezing and piling itself higher and higher. By January the drifts had filled the ravines and coulées almost level. The snow lay in great masses on the plateaus and river bottoms; and this lasted until the end of February. The preceding summer we had been visited by a prolonged drought, so that the short, scanty grass was already well cropped down; the snow covered what pasturage there was to the depth of several feet, and the cattle could not get at it at all, and could hardly move round. It was all but impossible to travel on horseback, except on a few well-beaten trails. It was dangerous to attempt to penetrate the Bad Lands, whose shape had been completely altered by the great white mounds and drifts. The starving cattle died by scores of thousands before their helpless owners' eyes. The bulls, the cows who were suckling calves, or who were heavy with calf, the weak cattle that had just been driven up on the trail, and the late calves suffered most; the old range animals did better, and the steers best of all; but the best was bad enough. Even many of the horses died. An outfit near me lost half its saddle-band, the animals having been worked so hard that they were very thin when fall came.

In the thick brush the stock got some shelter and sustenance. They gnawed every twig and bough they could get at. They browsed the bitter sage brush down to where the branches were the thickness of a man's finger. When near a ranch they crowded into the out-houses and sheds to die, and fences had to be built around the windows to keep the wild-eyed, desperate beasts from thrusting their heads through the glass panes. In most cases it was impossible either to drive them to the haystacks or to haul the hay out to them. The deer even were so weak as to be easily run down; and on one or two of the plateaus where there were bands of antelope, these wary creatures grew so numbed and feeble that they could have been slaughtered like rabbits. But the hunters could hardly get out, and could bring home neither hide nor meat, so the game went unharmed.

The way in which the cattle got through the winter depended largely on the different localities in which the bands were caught when the first heavy snows came. A group of animals in a bare valley, without underbrush and with steepish sides, would all die, weak and strong alike; they could get no food and no shelter, and so there would not be a hoof left. On the other hand, hundreds wintered on the great thickly wooded bottoms near my ranch house with little more than ordinary loss, though a skinny sorry-looking crew by the time the snow melted. In intermediate places the strong survived and the weak perished.

It would be impossible to imagine any sight more dreary and melancholy than that offered by the ranges when the snow went off in March. The land was a mere barren waste; not a green thing to be seen; the dead grass eaten off till the country looked as if it had been shaved with a razor. Occasionally among the desolate hills a rider would come across a band of gaunt, hollow-flanked cattle feebly cropping the sparse, dry pasturage, too listless to move out of the way; and the blackened carcasses lay in the sheltered spots, some stretched out, others in as natural a position as if the animals had merely lain down to rest. It was small wonder that cheerful stockmen were rare objects that spring. Our only comfort was that we did not, as usual, suffer a heavy loss from weak cattle getting mired down in the springs and mud-holes when the ice broke up — for all the weak animals were dead already. The truth is, ours is a primitive industry, and we suffer the reverses as well as enjoy the successes only known to primitive peoples. A hard winter is to us in the north what a dry summer is to Texas or Australia — what seasons of famine once were to all peoples. We still live in an iron age that the old civilized world has long passed by. The men of the border reckon upon stern and unending struggles with their iron-bound surroundings; against the grim harshness of their existence they set the strength and the abounding vitality that come with it. They run risks to life and limb that are unknown to the dwellers in cities; and what the men freely brave, the beasts that they own must also sometimes suffer.

Theodore Roosevelt.

50

CHAPTER FOUR

SHERIFF'S WORK ON A RANCH

A TEXAN COWBOY.

UP to 1880 the country through which the Little Missouri flows remained as wild and almost as unknown as it was when the old explorers and fur traders crossed it in the early part of the century. It was the last great Indian hunting-ground across which Grosventres and Mandans, Sioux and Cheyennes, and even Crows and Rees wandered in chase of game, and where they fought one another and plundered the small parties of white trappers and hunters that occasionally ventured into it. Once or twice generals like Sully and Custer had penetrated it in the course of the long, tedious, and bloody campaigns that finally broke the strength of the northern Horse Indians; indeed, the trail made by Custer's baggage train is to this day one of the well-known landmarks, for the deep ruts worn by the wheels of the heavy wagons are in many places still as distinctly to be seen as ever.

In 1883 a regular long-range skirmish took place just south of us between some Cheyennes and some cowboys, with bloodshed on both sides, while about the same time a band of Sioux plundered a party of buffalo hunters of everything they owned, and some Crows who attempted the same feat with another party were driven off with the loss of two of their number. Since then there have been in our neighborhood no stand-up fights or regular raids; but the Indians have at different times proved more or less troublesome, burning the grass, and occasionally killing stock or carrying off horses that have wandered some distance away. They have also themselves suffered somewhat at the hands of white horse-thieves.

Bands of them, accompanied by their squaws and children, often come into the ranch country, either to trade or to hunt, and are then, of course, perfectly meek and peaceable. If they stay any time they build themselves quite comfortable tepees (wigwams, as they would be styled in the East), and an Indian camp is a rather interesting, though very dirty, place to visit. On our ranch we get along particularly well with them, as it is a rule that they shall be treated as fairly as if they were whites: we neither wrong them ourselves nor allow others to wrong them. We have always, for example, been as keen in putting down horse-stealing from Indians as from whites — which indicates rather an advanced stage of frontier morality, as theft from the "redskins" or the "Government" is usually held to be a very trivial matter compared with the heinous crime of theft from "citizens."

There is always danger in meeting a band of young bucks in lonely, uninhabited country —those that have barely reached manhood being the most truculent, insolent, and reckless. A man meeting such a party runs great risk of losing his horse, his rifle, and all else he has. This has happened quite frequently during the past few years to hunters or cowboys who have wandered into the debatable territory where our country borders on the Indian lands; and in at least one such instance, that took place two years ago, the unfortunate individual lost his life as well as his belongings. But a frontiersman of any experience can generally "stand off" a small number of such assailants, unless he loses his nerve or is taken by surprise.

My only adventure with Indians was of a very mild kind. It was in the course of a solitary trip to the north and east of our range, to what was then practically unknown country, although now containing many herds of cattle. One morning I had been traveling along the edge of the prairie, and about noon I rode Manitou up a slight rise and came out on a plateau that was perhaps half a mile broad. When near the middle, four or five Indians suddenly came up over the edge, directly in front of me. The second they saw me they whipped their guns out of their slings, started their horses into a run, and came on at full tilt, whooping and brandishing their weapons. I instantly reined up and dismounted. The level plain where we were was of all places the one on which such an onslaught could best be

51

met. In any broken country, or where there is much cover, a white man is at a great disadvantage if pitted against such adepts in the art of hiding as Indians; while, on the other hand, the latter will rarely rush in on a foe who, even if overpowered in the end, will probably inflict severe loss on his assailants. The fury of an Indian charge, and the whoops by which it is accompanied, often scare horses so as to stampede them; but in Manitou I had perfect trust, and the old fellow stood as steady as a rock, merely cocking his ears and looking round at the noise. I waited until the Indians were a hundred yards off, and then threw up my rifle and drew a bead on the foremost. The effect was like magic. The whole party scattered out as wild pigeons or teal ducks sometimes do when shot at, and doubled back on their tracks, the men bending over alongside their horses. When some distance off they halted and gathered together to consult, and after a minute one came forward alone, ostentatiously dropping his rifle and waving a blanket over his head. When he came to within fifty yards I stopped him, and he pulled out a piece of paper — all Indians, when absent from their reservations, are supposed to carry passes — and called out, "How! Me good Indian!" I answered "How," and assured him most sincerely I was very glad he *was* a good Indian, but I would not let him come closer; and when his companions began to draw near, I covered him with the rifle and made him move off, which he did with a sudden lapse into the most canonical Anglo-Saxon profanity. I then started to lead my horse out to the prairie; and after hovering round a short time they rode off, while I followed suit, but in the opposite direction. It had all passed too quickly for me to have time to get frightened; but during the rest of my ride I was exceedingly uneasy, and pushed tough, speedy old Manitou along at a rapid rate, keeping well out on the level. However, I never saw the Indians again. They may not have intended any mischief beyond giving me a fright; but I did not dare to let them come to close quarters, for they would have probably taken my horse and rifle, and not impossibly my scalp as well. Towards nightfall I fell in with two old trappers who lived near Killdeer Mountains, and they informed me that my assailants were some young Sioux bucks, at whose hands they themselves had just suffered the loss of a couple of horses.

However, in our own immediate locality, we have had more difficulty with white desperadoes than with the redskins. At times there has been a good deal of cattle-killing and horse-stealing, and occasionally a murder or two. But as regards the last, a man has

very little more to fear in the West than in the East, in spite of all the lawless acts one reads about. Undoubtedly a long-standing quarrel sometimes ends in a shooting-match; and of course savage affrays occasionally take place in the barrooms; in which, be it remarked, that, inasmuch as the men are generally drunk, and, furthermore, as the revolver is at best a rather inaccurate weapon, outsiders are nearly as apt to get hurt as are the participants. But if a man minds his own business and does not go into barrooms, gambling saloons, and the like, he need have no fear of being molested; while a revolver is a mere foolish incumbrance for any but a trained expert, and need never be carried.

Against horse-thieves, cattle-thieves, claim-jumpers, and the like, however, every ranchman has to be on his guard; and armed collisions with these gentry are sometimes inevitable.

The fact of such scoundrels being able to ply their trade with impunity for any length of time can only be understood if the absolute wildness of our land is taken into account.

The country is yet unsurveyed and unmapped; the course of the river itself, as put down on the various Government and railroad maps, is very much a mere piece of guesswork, its bed being in many parts — as by my ranch — ten or fifteen miles, or more, away from where these maps make it.

White hunters came into the land by 1880; but the actual settlement only began in 1882, when the first cattle-men drove in their herds, all of Northern stock, the Texans not passing north of the country around the head-waters of the river until the following year, while until 1885 the territory through which it ran for the final hundred and fifty miles before entering the Big Missouri remained as little known as ever.

Some of us had always been anxious to run down the river in a boat during the time of the spring floods, as we thought we might get good duck and goose shooting, and also kill some beaver, while the trip would, in addition, have all the charm of an exploring expedition. Twice, so far as we knew, the feat had been performed, both times by hunters, and in one instance with very good luck in shooting and trapping. A third attempt, by a couple of men on a raft, made the spring preceding that on which we made ours, had been less successful; for when a score or so of miles below our ranch, a bear killed one of the two adventurers, and the survivor returned.

We could only go down during a freshet; for the Little Missouri, like most plains' rivers, is usually either a dwindling streamlet, a mere slender thread of sluggish water, or else a boiling, muddy torrent, running over a bed of shifting quicksand, that neither man nor beast can cross. It rises and falls with extraordinary suddenness and intensity; an instance of which has just occurred as this very page is being written. Last evening, when the moon rose, from the ranch veranda we could see the river-bed almost dry, the stream having shrunk under the drought till it was little but a string of shallow pools, with between them a trickle of water that was not ankle deep, and hardly wet the fetlocks of the saddle-band when driven across it; yet at daybreak this morning, without any rain having fallen near us, but doubtless in consequence of some heavy cloudburst near its head, the swift, swollen current was foaming brim high between the banks, and even the fords were swimming-deep for the horses.

Accordingly we had planned to run down the river sometime towards the end of April, taking advantage of a rise; but an accident made us start three or four weeks sooner than we had intended.

In 1886 the ice went out of the upper river very early, during the first part of February; but it at times almost froze over again, the bottom ice did not break up, and a huge gorge, scores of miles in length, formed in and above the bend known as the Ox-bow, a long distance up-stream from my ranch. About the middle of March this great Ox-bow jam came down past us. It moved slowly,

STANDING OFF INDIANS.

its front forming a high, crumbling wall, and creaming over like an immense breaker on the seashore: we could hear the dull roaring and crunching as it plowed down the river-bed long before it came in sight round the bend above us. The ice kept piling and tossing up in the middle, and not only heaped itself above the level of the banks, but also in many places spread out on each side beyond them, grinding against the cottonwood trees in front of the ranch veranda, and at one moment bidding fair to overwhelm the house itself. It did not, however, but moved slowly down past us with that look of vast, resistless, relentless force that any great body of moving ice, as a glacier, or an iceberg, always conveys to the beholder. The heaviest pressure from the water that was backed up behind being, of course, always in the middle, this part kept breaking away, and finally was pushed on clear through, leaving the river so changed that it could hardly be known. On each

53

bank, and for a couple of hundred feet out from it into the stream, was a solid mass of ice, edging the river along most of its length, at least as far as its course lay through lands that we knew; and in the narrow channel between the sheer ice-walls the water ran like a mill-race.

At night the snowy, glittering masses, tossed

ONE OF THE BOYS.

and heaped up into fantastic forms, shone like crystal in the moonlight; but they soon lost their beauty, becoming fouled and blackened, and at the same time melted and settled down until it was possible to clamber out across the slippery hummocks.

We had brought out a clinker-built boat especially to ferry ourselves over the river when it was high, and were keeping our ponies on the opposite side, where there was a good range shut in by some very broken country that we knew they would not be apt to cross. This boat had already proved very useful and now came in handier than ever, as without it we could take no care of our horses. We kept it on the bank tied to a tree, and every day would carry it or slide it across the hither ice bank, usually with not a little tumbling and scrambling on our part, lower it gently into the swift current, pole it across to the ice on the farther bank, and then drag it over that, repeating the operation when we came back. One day we crossed and walked off about ten miles to a tract of wild and rugged country, cleft in every direction by ravines and cedar canyons, in the deepest of which we had left four deer hanging a fortnight before, as game thus hung up in cold weather keeps indefinitely. The walking was

very bad, especially over the clay buttes; for the sun at midday had enough strength to thaw out the soil to the depth of a few inches only, and accordingly the steep hillsides were covered by a crust of slippery mud, with the frozen ground underneath. It was hard to keep one's footing, and to avoid falling while balancing along the knife-like ridge crests, or while clinging to the stunted sage brush as we went down into the valleys. The deer had been hung in a thicket of dwarfed cedars; but when we reached the place we found nothing save scattered pieces of their carcasses, and the soft mud was tramped all over with round, deeply marked footprints, some of them but a few hours old, showing that the plunderers of our cache were a pair of cougars —"mountain lions," as they are called by the Westerners. They had evidently been at work for some time, and had eaten almost every scrap of flesh; one of the deer had been carried for some distance to the other side of a deep, narrow, chasm-like gully across which the cougar must have leaped with the carcass in its mouth. We followed the fresh trail of the cougars for some time, as it was well marked, especially in the snow still remaining in the bottoms of the deeper ravines; finally it led into a tangle of rocky hills riven by dark cedar-clad gorges, in which we lost it, and we retraced our steps, intending to return on the morrow with a good track hound.

But we never carried out our intentions, for next morning one of my men who was out before breakfast came back to the house with the startling news that our boat was gone — stolen, for he brought with him the end of the rope with which it had been tied, evidently cut off with a sharp knife; and also a red woolen mitten with a leather palm, which he had picked up on the ice. We had no doubt as to who had stolen it; for whoever had done so had certainly gone down the river in it, and the only other thing in the shape of a boat on the Little Missouri was a small flat-bottomed scow in the possession of three hard characters who lived in a shack or hut some twenty miles above us, and whom we had shrewdly suspected for some time of wishing to get out of the country, as certain of the cattle-men had begun openly to threaten to lynch them. They belonged to a class that always holds sway during the raw youth of a frontier community, and the putting down of which is the first step towards decent government. Dakota, west of the Missouri, has been settled very recently, and every town within it has seen strange antics performed during the past five or six years. Medora, in particular, has had more than its full share of shooting and stabbing affrays, horse-stealing and cattle-killing.

But the time for such things was passing away; and during the preceding fall the vigilantes—locally known as "stranglers," in happy allusion to their summary method of doing justice—had made a clean sweep of the cattle country along the Yellowstone and that part of the Big Missouri around and below its mouth. Be it remarked, in passing, that while the outcome of their efforts had been in the main wholesome, yet, as is always the case in an extended raid of vigilantes, several of the sixty odd victims had been perfectly innocent men who had been hung or shot in company with the real scoundrels, either through carelessness and misapprehension or on account of some personal spite.

case, and had been chief actor in a number of shooting scrapes. The other two were a half-breed, a stout, muscular man, and an old German, whose viciousness was of the weak and shiftless type.

We knew that these three men were becoming uneasy and were anxious to leave the locality; and we also knew that traveling on horseback, in the direction in which they would wish to go, was almost impossible, as the swollen, ice-fringed rivers could not be crossed at all, and the stretches of broken ground would form nearly as impassable barriers. So we had little doubt that it was they who had taken our boat; and as they knew there was then no boat left on the river, and

MOUNTAIN LIONS AT THE DEER CACHE.

The three men we suspected had long been accused—justly or unjustly—of being implicated both in cattle-killing and in that worst of frontier crimes, horse-stealing: it was only by an accident that they had escaped the clutches of the vigilantes the preceding fall. Their leader was a well-built fellow named Finnigan, who had long red hair reaching to his shoulders, and always wore a broad hat and a fringed buckskin shirt. He was rather a hard

as the country along its banks was entirely impracticable for horses, we felt sure they would be confident that there could be no pursuit.

Accordingly we at once set to work in our turn to build a flat-bottomed scow, wherein to follow them. Our loss was very annoying, and might prove a serious one if we were long prevented from crossing over to look after the saddle-band; but the determining motive in our minds was neither chagrin nor anxiety to recover our property. In any wild country where the power of the law is little felt or heeded, and where every one has to rely upon himself for protection, men soon get to feel that it is in the highest degree unwise to submit to any wrong without making an immediate and resolute effort to avenge it upon the wrong-doers, at no matter what cost of risk or trouble. To submit tamely and meekly to theft, or to any other injury, is to invite almost certain repetition of the offense, in a place where self-reliant hardihood and the ability to hold one's own under all circumstances rank as the first of virtues.

Two of my cowboys, Seawall and Dow, were originally from Maine, and were mighty men of their hands, skilled in woodcraft and the use of the ax, paddle, and rifle. They set to work with a will, and, as by good luck there were plenty of boards, in two or three days they had turned out a first-class flat-bottom, which was roomy, drew very little water, and was dry as a bone; and though, of course, not a handy craft, was easily enough managed in going down-stream. Into this we packed flour, coffee, and bacon enough to last us a fortnight or so, plenty of warm bedding, and the mess kit; and early one cold March morning slid it into the icy current, took our seats, and shoved off down the river.

There could have been no better men for a trip of this kind than my two companions, Seawall and Dow. They were tough, hardy, resolute fellows, quick as cats, strong as bears, and able to travel like bull moose. We felt very little uneasiness as to the result of a fight with the men we were after, provided we had anything like a fair show; moreover, we intended, if possible, to get them at such a disadvantage that there would not be any fight at all. The only risk of any consequence that we ran was that of being ambushed; for the extraordinary formation of the Bad Lands, with the ground cut up into gullies, serried walls, and battlemented hilltops, makes it the country of all others for hiding-places and ambuscades.

For several days before we started the weather had been bitterly cold, as a furious blizzard was blowing; but on the day we left there was a lull, and we hoped a thaw had set in. We all were most warmly and thickly dressed, with woolen socks and underclothes, heavy jackets and trousers, and great fur coats, so that we felt we could bid defiance to the weather. Each carried his rifle, and we had in addition a double-barreled duck gun, for water-fowl and beaver. To manage the boat, we had paddles, heavy oars, and long iron-shod poles, Seawall steering

while Dow sat in the bow. Altogether we felt as if we were off on a holiday trip, and set to work to have as good a time as possible.

The river twisted in every direction, winding to and fro across the alluvial valley bottom, only to be brought up by the rows of great barren buttes that bounded it on each edge. It had worn away the sides of these till they towered up as cliffs of clay, marl, or sandstone. Across their white faces the seams of coal drew sharp black bands, and they were elsewhere blotched and varied with brown, yellow, purple, and red. This fantastic coloring, together with the jagged irregularity of their crests, channeled by the weather into spires, buttresses, and battlements, as well as their barrenness and the distinctness with which they loomed up through the high, dry air, gave them a look that was a singular mixture of the terrible and the grotesque. The bottoms were covered thickly with leafless cottonwood trees, or else with withered brown grass and stunted, sprawling sage bushes. At times the cliffs rose close to us on either hand, and again the valley would widen into a sinuous oval a mile or two long, bounded on every side, as far as our eyes could see, by a bluff line without a break, until, as we floated down close to its other end, there would suddenly appear in one corner a cleft through which the stream rushed out. As it grew dusk the shadowy outlines of the buttes lost nothing of their weirdness; the twilight only made their uncouth shapelessness more grim and forbidding. They looked like the crouching figures of great goblin beasts.

> Those two hills on the right
> Crouched like two bulls locked horn in horn in fight—
> While to the left a tall scalped mountain. . . .
> The dying sunset kindled through a cleft:
> The hills, like giants at a hunting, lay
> Chin upon hand, to see the game at bay—

might well have been written after seeing the strange, desolate lands lying in western Dakota.

All through the early part of the day we drifted swiftly down between the heaped-up piles of ice, the cakes and slabs now dirty and unattractive looking. Towards evening, however, there came long reaches where the banks on either side were bare, though even here there would every now and then be necks where the jam had been crowded into too narrow a spot and had risen over the side as it had done up-stream, grinding the bark from the big cottonwoods and snapping the smaller ones short off. In such places the ice-walls were sometimes eight or ten feet high, continually undermined by the restless current; and every now and then overhanging pieces would break off and slide into the stream with a loud sullen splash, like the plunge of some great water beast. Nor did we dare to go in too close to the high cliffs, as bowlders and earth masses, freed by the thaw from the grip of the frost, kept rolling and leaping down their faces and forced us to keep a sharp look-out lest our boat should be swamped.

At nightfall we landed, and made our camp on a point of wood-covered land jutting out into the stream. We had seen very little trace of life until late in the day, for the ducks had not yet arrived; but in the afternoon a sharp-tailed prairie fowl flew across stream ahead of the boat, lighting on a low branch by the water's edge. Shooting him, we landed and picked off two others that were perched high up in leafless cottonwoods, plucking the buds. These three birds served us as supper; and shortly afterward, as the cold grew more and more biting, we rolled in under our furs and blankets and were soon asleep.

In the morning it was evident that instead of thawing it had grown decidedly colder. The anchor ice was running thick in the river, and we spent the first hour or two after sunrise in hunting over the frozen swamp bottom for white-tail deer, of which there were many tracks; but we saw nothing. Then we broke camp — a simple operation, as we had no tent, and all we had to do was to cord up our bedding and gather the mess kit — and again started down-stream. It was colder than before, and for some time we went along in chilly silence, nor was it until midday that the sun warmed our blood in the least. The crooked bed of the current twisted hither and thither, but whichever way it went the icy north wind, blowing stronger all the time, drew steadily up it. One of us remarking that we bade fair to have it in our faces all day, the steersman announced that we could n't, unless it was the crookedest wind in Dakota; and half an hour afterward we overheard him muttering to himself that it *was* the crookedest wind in Dakota. We passed a group of tepees on one bottom, marking the deserted winter camp of some Grosventre Indians, which some of my men had visited a few months previously on a trading expedition. It was almost the last point on the river with which we were acquainted. At midday we landed on a sand-bar for lunch; a simple enough meal, the tea being boiled over a fire of driftwood, that also fried the bacon, while the bread only needed to be baked every other day. Then we again shoved off. As the afternoon waned the cold grew still more bitter, and the wind increased, blow-

ing in fitful gusts against us, until it chilled us to the marrow when we sat still. But we rarely did sit still; for even the rapid current was unable to urge the light-draught scow down in the teeth of the strong blasts, and we only got her along by dint of hard work with pole and paddle. Long before the sun went down the ice had begun to freeze on the handles of the poles, and we were not sorry to haul on shore for the night. For supper we again had prairie fowl, having shot four from a great patch of bulberry bushes late in the afternoon. A man doing hard open-air work in cold weather is always hungry for meat.

During the night the thermometer went down to zero, and in the morning the anchor ice was running so thickly that we did not care to start at once, for it is most difficult to handle a boat in the deep frozen slush. Accordingly we took a couple of hours for a deer hunt, as there were evidently many white-tail on the bottom. We selected one long, isolated patch of tangled trees and brushwood, two of us beating through it while the other watched one end; but almost before we had begun four deer broke out at one side, loped easily off, evidently not much scared, and took refuge in a deep glen or gorge, densely wooded with cedars, that made a blind pocket in the steep side of one of the great plateaus bounding the bottom. After a short consultation, one of our number crept round to the head of the gorge, making a wide détour, and the other two advanced up it on each side, thus completely surrounding the doomed deer. They attempted to break out past the man at the head of the glen, who shot down a couple, a buck and a yearling doe. The other two made their escape by running off over ground so rough that it looked fitter to be crossed by their upland-loving cousins, the black-tail.

THE CAPTURE OF THE GERMAN.

57

This success gladdened our souls, insuring us plenty of fresh meat. We carried pretty much all of both deer back to camp, and, after a hearty breakfast, loaded our scow and started merrily off once more. The cold still continued intense, and as the day wore away we became numbed by it, until at last an incident occurred that set our blood running freely again.

terest, for the capture itself was as tame as possible.

The men we were after knew they had taken with them the only craft there was on the river, and so felt perfectly secure; accordingly, we took them absolutely by surprise. The only one in camp was the German, whose weapons were on the ground, and who, of course, gave up at

"HANDS UP!"—THE CAPTURE OF FINNIGAN.

We were, of course, always on the alert, keeping a sharp lookout ahead and around us, and making as little noise as possible. Finally our watchfulness was rewarded, for in the middle of the afternoon of this, the third day we had been gone, as we came round a bend, we saw in front of us the lost boat, together with a scow, moored against the bank, while from among the bushes some little way back the smoke of a camp-fire curled up through the frosty air. We had come on the camp of the thieves. As I glanced at the faces of my two followers I was struck by the grim, eager look in their eyes. Our overcoats were off in a second, and after exchanging a few muttered words, the boat was hastily and silently shoved towards the bank. As soon as it touched the shore ice I leaped out and ran up behind a clump of bushes, so as to cover the landing of the others, who had to make the boat fast. For a moment we felt a thrill of keen excitement, and our veins tingled as we crept cautiously towards the fire, for it seemed likely there would be a brush; but, as it turned out, this was almost the only moment of much in-

once, his two companions being off hunting. We made him safe, delegating one of our number to look after him particularly and see that he made no noise, and then sat down and waited for the others. The camp was under the lee of a cut bank, behind which we crouched, and, after waiting an hour or over, the men we were after came in. We heard them a long way off and made ready, watching them for some minutes as they walked towards us, their rifles on their shoulders and the sunlight glinting on the steel barrels. When they were within twenty yards or so we straightened up from behind the bank, covering them with our cocked rifles, while I shouted to them to hold up their hands — an order that in such a case, in the West, a man is not apt to disregard if he thinks the giver is in earnest. The half-breed obeyed at once, his knees trembling as if they had been made of whalebone. Finnigan hesitated for a second, his eyes fairly wolfish; then, as I walked up within a few paces, covering the center of his chest so as to avoid overshooting, and repeating the command, he saw he had no show, and, with an oath,

"TAKE OFF YOUR BOOTS!"

let his rifle drop and held his hands up beside his head.

It was nearly dusk, so we camped where we were. The first thing to be done was to collect enough wood to enable us to keep a blazing fire all night long. While Seawall and Dow, thoroughly at home in the use of the ax, chopped down dead cottonwood trees and dragged the logs up into a huge pile, I kept guard over the three prisoners, who were huddled into a sullen group some twenty yards off, just the right distance for the buckshot in the double-barrel. Having captured our men, we were in a quandary how to keep them. The cold was so intense that to tie them tightly hand and foot meant, in all likelihood, freezing both hands and feet off during the night; and it was no use tying them at all unless we tied them tightly enough to stop in part the circulation. So nothing was left for us to do but to keep perpetual guard over them. Of course we had carefully searched them, and taken away not only their firearms and knives, but everything else that could possibly be used as a weapon. By this time they were pretty well cowed, as they found out very quickly that they would be well treated so long as they remained quiet, but would receive some rough handling if they attempted any disturbance.

Our next step was to cord their weapons up in some bedding, which we sat on while we took supper. Immediately afterward we made the men take off their boots — an additional safeguard, as it was a cactus country, in which a man could travel barefoot only at the risk of almost certainly laming himself for life — and go to bed, all three lying on one buffalo robe and being covered by another, in the full light of the blazing fire. We determined to watch in succession a half-night apiece, thus each getting a full rest every third night. I took first watch, my two companions, revolver under head, rolling up in their blankets on the side of the fire opposite that on which the three captives lay; while I, in fur cap, gantlets, and overcoat, took my station a little way back in the circle of firelight, in a position in which I could watch my men with the absolute certainty of being able to stop any movement, no matter how sudden. For this night-watching we always used the double-barrel with buckshot, as a rifle is uncertain in the dark; while with a shot-gun at such a distance, and with men lying down, a person who is watchful may be sure that they cannot get up, no matter how quick they are, without being riddled. The only danger lies in the extreme monotony of sitting still in the dark guarding men who make no motion, and the consequent tendency to go to sleep, especially when one has had a hard day's work and is feeling really tired. But neither on the first night nor on any subsequent one did we ever abate a jot of our watchfulness.

59

Next morning we started down-stream, having a well-laden flotilla, for the men we had caught had a good deal of plunder in their boats, including some saddles, as they evidently intended to get horses as soon as they reached a part of the country where there were any, and where it was possible to travel. Finnigan, who was the ringleader, and the man I was especially after, I kept by my side in our boat, the other two being put in their own scow, heavily laden and rather leaky, and with only one paddle. We kept them just in front of us, a few yards distant, the river being so broad that we knew, and they knew also, any attempt at escape to be perfectly hopeless.

For some miles we went swiftly down-stream, the cold being bitter and the slushy anchor ice choking the space between the boats; then the current grew sluggish, eddies forming along the sides. We paddled on until, coming into a long reach where the water was almost backed up, we saw there was a stoppage at the other end. Working up to this, it proved to be a small ice jam, through which we broke our way only to find ourselves, after a few hundred yards, stopped by another. We had hoped that the first was merely a jam of anchor ice, caused by the cold of the last few days; but the jam we had now come to was black and solid, and, running the boats ashore, one of us went off down the bank to find out what the matter was. On climbing a hill that commanded a view of the valley for several miles, the explanation became only too evident — as far as we could see, the river was choked with black ice. The great Ox-bow jam had stopped and we had come down to its tail.

We had nothing to do but to pitch camp, after which we held a consultation. The Little Missouri has much too swift a current,— when it has any current at all,— with too bad a bottom, for it to be possible to take a boat up-stream; and to walk, of course, meant abandoning almost all we had. Moreover we knew that a thaw would very soon start the jam, and so made up our minds that we had best simply stay where we were, and work down-stream as fast as we could, trusting that the spell of bitter weather would pass before our food gave out.

The next eight days were as irksome and monotonous as any I ever spent: there is very little amusement in combining the functions of a sheriff with those of an arctic explorer. The weather kept as cold as ever. During the night the water in the pail would freeze solid. Ice formed all over the river, thickly along the banks; and the clear, frosty sun gave us so little warmth that the melting hardly began before noon. Each day the great jam would settle down-stream a few miles, only to wedge again, leaving behind it several smaller jams, through which we would work our way until we were as close to the tail of the large one as we dared to go.

We had to be additionally cautious on account of being in the Indian country, having worked down past Killdeer Mountains, where some of my cowboys had run across a band of Sioux — said to be Tetons — the year before. Very probably the Indians would not have harmed us anyhow, but as we were hampered by the prisoners, we preferred not meeting them; nor did we, though we saw plenty of fresh signs, and found, to our sorrow, that they had just made a grand hunt all down the river, and had killed or driven off almost every head of game in the country through which we were passing. As our stock of provisions grew scantier and scant-

ON GUARD AT NIGHT.

ier, we tried in vain to eke it out by the chase; for we saw no game. Two of us would go out hunting at a time, while the third kept guard over the prisoners. The latter would be made to sit down together on a blanket at one side of the fire, while the guard for the time being stood or sat some fifteen or twenty yards off. The prisoners being un-

We broke camp in the morning, on a point of land covered with brown, leafless, frozen cottonwoods; and in the afternoon we pitched camp on another point in the midst of a grove of the same stiff, dreary trees. The discolored river, whose eddies boiled into yellow foam, flowed always between the same banks of frozen mud or of muddy ice. And what

DOWN-STREAM.

armed, and kept close together, there was no possibility of their escaping, and the guard kept at such a distance that they could not overpower him by springing on him, he having a Winchester or the double-barreled shot-gun always in his hands cocked and at the ready. So long as we kept wide-awake and watchful, there was not the least danger, as our three men knew us, and understood perfectly that the slightest attempt at a break would result in their being shot down; but, although there was thus no risk, it was harassing, tedious work, and the strain, day in and day out, without any rest or let up, became very tiresome.

The days were monotonous to a degree. The endless rows of hills bounding the valley, barren and naked, stretched along without a break. When we rounded a bend, it was only to see on each hand the same lines of broken buttes dwindling off into the distance ahead of us as they had dwindled off into the distance behind. If, in hunting, we climbed to their tops, as far as our eyes could scan there was nothing but the great rolling prairie, bleak and lifeless, reaching off to the horizon.

was, from a practical standpoint, even worse, our diet began to be as same as the scenery. Being able to kill nothing, we exhausted all our stock of provisions and got reduced to flour, without yeast or baking-powder; and unleavened bread, made with exceedingly muddy water, is not, as a steady thing, attractive.

Finding that they were well treated and were also watched with the closest vigilance, our prisoners behaved themselves excellently and gave no trouble, though afterward, when out of our hands and shut up in jail, the halfbreed got into a stabbing affray. They conversed freely with my two men on a number of indifferent subjects, and after the first evening no allusion was made to the theft, or anything connected with it; so that an outsider overhearing the conversation would never have guessed what our relations to each other really were. Once, and once only, did Finnigan broach the subject. Somebody had been speaking of a man whom we all knew, known as "Calamity," who had been recently taken by the sheriff on a charge of horsestealing. Calamity had escaped once, but was caught at a disadvantage the next time;

61

"A SHARP PRELIMINARY TUSSLE."

nevertheless, when summoned to hold his hands up, he refused, and attempted to draw his own revolver, with the result of having two bullets put through him. Finnigan commented on Calamity as a fool for "not knowing when a man had the drop on him"; and then, suddenly turning to me, said, his weather-beaten face flashing darkly: "If I'd had any show at all, you'd have sure had to fight, Mr. Roosevelt; but there wasn't any use making a break when I'd only have got shot myself, with no chance of harming any one else." I laughed and nodded, and the subject was dropped.

Indeed, if the time was tedious to us, it must have seemed never-ending to our prisoners, who had nothing to do but to lie still and read, or chew the bitter cud of their reflections, always conscious that some pair of eyes was watching them every moment, and that at least one loaded rifle was ever ready to be used against them. They had quite a stock of books, some of a rather unexpected kind. Dime novels and the inevitable "History of the James Brothers"—a book that, together with the "Police Gazette," is to be found in the hands of every professed or putative ruffian in the West—seemed perfectly in place; but it was somewhat surprising to find that a large number of more or less drearily silly "society" novels, ranging from Ouida's to those of The Duchess and Augusta J. Evans, were most greedily devoured.

Our commons grew shorter and shorter; and finally even the flour was nearly gone, and we were again forced to think seriously of abandoning the boats. The Indians had driven all the deer out of the country; occasionally we shot prairie fowl, but they were not plentiful. A flock of geese passed us one morning, and afterward an old gander settled down on the river near our camp; but he was over two hundred yards off, and a rifle-shot missed him.

But when the day was darkest the dawn appeared. At last, having worked down some thirty miles at the tail of the ice jam, we struck an outlying cow-camp of the C Diamond (C ◇) ranch, and knew that our troubles were almost over. There was but one cowboy in it, but we were certain of his cordial help, for in a stock country all make common cause against either horse-thieves or cattle-thieves. He had no wagon, but told us we could get one up at a ranch near Killdeer Mountains, some fifteen miles off, and lent me a pony to go up there and see about it — which I accordingly did, after a sharp preliminary tussle when I came to mount the wiry bronco. When I reached the solitary ranch spoken of, I was able to hire a large prairie schooner and two tough little bronco mares, driven by the settler himself, a rugged old plainsman, who evidently could hardly understand why I took so much bother with the thieves instead of hanging them off-hand. Returning to the river the next day, we walked our men up to the Killdeer Mountains. Seawall and Dow left me the following morning, went back to the boats, and had no further difficulty, for the weather set in very warm, the ice went through with a rush, and they reached Mandan in about ten days, killing four beaver and five geese on the way, but lacking time to stop and do any regular hunting.

Meanwhile I took the three thieves in to with them, except for the driver, of whom I knew nothing, I had to be doubly on my guard, and never let them come close to me. The little mares went so slowly, and the heavy road rendered any hope of escape by flogging up the horses so entirely out of the question, that I soon found the safest plan was to put the prisoners in the wagon and myself walk behind with the inevitable Winchester. Accordingly I trudged steadily the whole time behind the wagon through the ankle-deep mud. It was a gloomy walk. Hour after hour went by always the same, while I plodded along through the dreary landscape — hunger,

ON THE ROAD TO DICKINSON.

Dickinson, the nearest town. The going was bad, and the little mares could only drag the wagon at a walk, so, though we drove during the daylight, it took us two days and a night to make the journey. It was a most desolate drive. The prairie had been burned the fall before, and was a mere bleak waste of blackened earth, and a cold, rainy mist lasted throughout the two days. The only variety was where the road crossed the shallow headwaters of Knife and Green rivers. Here the ice was high along the banks, and the wagon had to be taken to pieces to get it over. My three captives were unarmed, but as I was alone cold, and fatigue struggling with a sense of dogged, weary resolution. At night, when we put up at the squalid hut of a frontier granger, the only habitation on our road, it was even worse. I did not dare to go to sleep, but making my three men get into the upper bunk, from which they could get out only with difficulty, I sat up with my back against the cabin-door and kept watch over them all night long. So, after thirty-six hours' sleeplessness, I was most heartily glad when we at last jolted into the long, straggling main street of Dickinson, and I was able to give my unwilling companions into the hands of the sheriff.

Theodore Roosevelt.

63

CHAPTER FIVE

THE RANCHMAN'S RIFLE
ON CRAG AND PRAIRIE

THE TEXAS TYPE OF COWBOY.

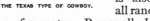

THE ranchman owes to his rifle not only the keen pleasure and strong excitement of the chase, but also much of his bodily comfort; for, save for his prowess as a hunter and his skill as a marksman with this, his favorite weapon, he would almost always be sadly stinted for fresh meat. Now that the buffalo have gone, and the Sharps rifle by which they were destroyed is also gone, almost all ranchmen use some form of repeater. Personally I prefer the Winchester, using the new model, with a 45-caliber bullet of 300 grains, backed by 90 grains of powder.

From April to August antelope are the game we chiefly follow, killing only the bucks; after that season, black-tail and white-tail deer. Occasionally we kill white-tail by driving them out of the wooded bottoms with the help of the slow, bell-mouthed, keen-nosed Southern track-hounds; or more often take the swift gazehounds and, on the open prairie, by sheer speed, run down antelope, jack-rabbit, coyotes, and foxes. Now and then we get a chance at mountain sheep, and more rarely at larger game still. As a rule, I never shoot anything but bucks. But in the rutting season, when the bucks' flesh is poor, or when we need to lay in a good stock of meat for the winter, this rule of course must be broken.

A small band of elk yet linger round a great patch of prairie and Bad Lands some thirty-five miles off. In 1885 I killed a good bull out of the lot; and once last season, when we were sorely in need of meat for smoking and drying, we went after them again. At the time most of the ponies were off on one of the round-ups, which indeed I had myself just left. However, my two hunting-horses, Manitou and Sorrel Joe, were at home. The former I rode myself, and on the latter I mounted one of my men

who was a particularly good hand at finding and following game. With much difficulty we got together a scrub wagon team of four as unkempt, dejected, and vicious-looking broncos as ever stuck fast in a quicksand or balked in pulling up a steep pitch. Their driver was a crack whip, and their load light, consisting of little but the tent and the bedding; so we got out to the hunting-ground and back in safety; but as the river was high and the horses were weak, we came within an ace of being swamped at one crossing, and the country was so very rough that we were only able to get the wagon up the worst pitch by hauling from the saddle with the riding-animals.

We camped by an excellent spring of cold, clear water — not a common luxury in the Bad Lands. We pitched the tent beside it, getting enough timber from a grove of ash to make a large fire, which again is an appreciated blessing on the plains of the West, where we often need to carry along with us the wood for cooking our supper and breakfast, and sometimes actually have to dig up our fuel, making the fire of sage-brush roots, eked out with buffalo chips. Though the days were still warm, the nights were frosty. Our camp was in a deep valley, bounded by steep hills with sloping, grassy sides, one of them marked by a peculiar shelf of rock. The country for miles was of this same character, much broken, but everywhere passable for horsemen, and with the hills rounded and grassy, except now and then for a chain of red scoria buttes or an isolated sugar-loaf cone of gray and brown clay. The first day we spent in trying to find the probable locality of our game; and after beating pretty thoroughly over the smoother country, towards nightfall we found quite fresh elk tracks leading into a stretch of very rough and broken land about ten miles from camp.

We started next morning before the gray was relieved by the first faint flush of pink, and reached the broken country soon after sunrise. Here we dismounted and picketed our horses, as the ground we were to hunt through was very rough. Two or three hours passed before we came upon fresh signs of elk. Then we found the trails that two, from the size presumably cows, had made the preceding night, and started to follow them, carefully and noiselessly, my companion taking one side of the valley in which we were, and I the other. The tracks led into one of the wildest and most desolate parts of the Bad Lands. It was now the heat of the day, the brazen sun shining out of a cloudless sky, and not the least breeze stirring. At the bottom of the

could, the game must have heard or smelt us; for after a mile's painstaking search we came to a dense thicket in which were two beds, evidently but just left, for the twigs and bent grass-blades were still slowly rising from the ground to which the bodies of the elk had pressed them. The long, clean hoof-prints told us that the quarry had started off at a

OUR ELK OUTFIT AT THE FORD.

valley, in the deep, narrow bed of the winding water-course, lay a few tepid little pools, almost dried up. Thick groves of stunted cedars stood here and there in the glen-like pockets of the high buttes, the peaks and sides of which were bare, and only their lower, terrace-like ledges thinly clad with coarse, withered grass and sprawling sage-bush; the parched hill-sides were riven by deep, twisting gorges, with brushwood in the bottoms; and the cliffs of coarse clay were cleft and seamed by sheer-sided, canyon-like gullies. In the narrow ravines, closed in by barren, sun-baked walls, the hot air stood still and sultry; the only living beings were the rattlesnakes, and of these I have never elsewhere seen so many. Some basked in the sun, stretched out at their ugly length of mottled brown and yellow; others lay half under stones or twined in the roots of the sage-brush, and looked straight at me with that strange, sullen, evil gaze, never shifting or moving, that is the property only of serpents and of certain men; while one or two coiled and rattled menacingly as I stepped near.

Yet, though we walked as quietly as we

swinging trot. We followed at once, and it was wonderful to see how such large, heavy beasts had gone up the steepest hill-sides without altering their swift and easy gait, and had plunged unhesitatingly over nearly sheer cliffs down which we had to clamber with careful slowness.

They left the strip of rugged Bad Lands and went on into the smoother country beyond, luckily passing quite close to where our horses were picketed. We thought it likely they would halt in some heavily timbered coulies six or seven miles off, and as there was no need of hurry, we took lunch and then began following them up — an easy feat, as their hoofs had sunk deep into the soft soil, the prints of the dew-claws showing now and then. At first we rode, but soon dismounted, and led our horses.

We found the elk almost as soon as we struck the border of the ground we had marked as their probable halting-place. Our horses were unshod and made but little noise; and coming to a wide, long coulie, filled with tall trees and brushwood, we as usual separated, I

65

going down one side and my companion the other. When nearly half-way down he suddenly whistled sharply, and I of course at once stood still, with my rifle at the ready. Nothing moved, and I glanced at him. He had squatted down and was gazing earnestly over into the dense laurel on my side of the coulie. In a minute he shouted that he saw a red patch in the brush which he thought must be the elk, and that it was right between him and myself. Elk will sometimes lie as closely as rabbits, even when not in very good cover; still I was a little surprised at these not breaking out when they heard human voices. However, there they staid; and I waited several minutes in vain for them to move. From where I stood it was impossible to see them, and I was fearful that they might go off down the valley and so offer me a very poor shot. Meanwhile, Manitou, who is not an emotional horse, and

OUR CAMP.

is moreover blessed with a large appetite, was feeding greedily, rattling his bridle-chains at every mouthful; and I thought he would act as a guard to keep the elk where they were until I shifted my position. So I slipped back, and ran swiftly round the head of the coulie to where my companion was still sitting. He pointed me out the patch of red in the bushes, not sixty yards distant, and I fired into it without delay, by good luck breaking the neck of a cow elk, when immediately another one rose up from beside it and made off. I had five shots at her as she ascended the hill-side and the gentle slope beyond; and two of my bullets struck her close together in the flank, ranging forward—a very fatal shot. She was evidently mortally hit, and just as she reached the top of the divide she stopped, reeled, and fell over, dead.

We were much pleased with our luck, as it

secured us an ample stock of needed fresh meat; and the two elk lay very handily, so that on the following day we were able to stop for them with the wagon on our way homeward, putting them in bodily, and leaving only the entrails for the vultures that were already soaring in great circles over the carcasses.

In the fall of 1886 I went far west to the Rockies and took a fortnight's hunting trip among the northern spurs of the Cœur d'Alêne, between the towns of Heron and Horseplains in Montana. There are many kinds of game to be found in the least known or still untrodden parts of this wooded mountain wilderness—caribou, elk, ungainly moose with great shovel horns, cougars, and bears. But I did not have time to go deeply into the heart of the forest-clad ranges, and devoted my entire energies to the chase of but one animal, the white antelope-goat, at present the least known and rarest of all American game.

We started from one of those most dismal and forlorn of all places, a dead mining town, on the line of the Northern Pacific Railroad. My foreman, Merrifield, was with me, and as guide I took a tall, lithe, happy-go-lucky mountaineer, who, like so many of the restless frontier race, was born in Missouri. Our outfit was simple, as we carried only blankets, a light wagon sheet, the ever-present camera, flour, bacon, salt, sugar, and coffee; canned goods are very unhandy to pack about on horseback. Our rifles and ammunition, with the few cooking-utensils and a book or two, completed the list. Four solemn ponies and a ridiculous little mule named Walla Walla bore us and our belongings. The Missourian was an expert packer, versed in the mysteries of the "diamond hitch," the only arrangement of the ropes that will insure a load staying in its place. Driving a pack train through the wooded paths and up the mountain passes that we had to traverse is hard work anyhow, as there are sure to be accidents happening to the animals all the time, while their packs receive rough treatment from jutting rocks and overhanging branches, or from the half-fallen tree-trunks under which the animals wriggle; and if the loads are continually coming loose, or slipping so as to gall the horses' backs and make them sore, the labor and anxiety are increased tenfold.

In a day or two we were in the heart of the vast wooded wilderness. A broad, lonely river ran through its midst, cleaving asunder the

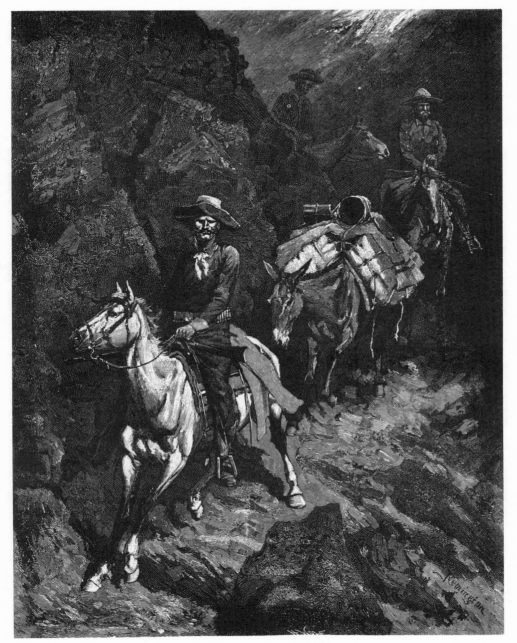

IN A CANYON OF THE CŒUR D'ALÊNE.

67

mountain chains. Range after range, peak upon peak, the mountains towered on every side, the lower timbered to the top, the higher with bare crests of gray crags or else hooded with fields of shining snow. The deep valleys lay half in darkness, hemmed in by steep, timbered slopes and straight rock walls. The torrents, broken into glittering foam masses, sprang down through the chasms they had rent in the sides of the high hills, lingered in black pools under the shadows of the scarred cliffs, and reaching the rank, tree-choked valleys, gathered into rapid streams of clear brown water, that drenched the drooping limbs of the tangled alders. Over the whole land lay like a shroud the mighty growth of the unbroken evergreen forest — spruce and hemlock, fir, balsam, tamarack, and lofty pine.

Yet even these vast wastes of shadowy woodland were once penetrated by members of that adventurous and now fast vanishing folk, the American frontiersmen. Once or twice, while walking silently over the spongy moss beneath the somber archways of the pines, we saw on a tree-trunk a dim, faint ax-scar, the bark almost grown over it, showing

and eager. There is no plain so lonely that their feet have not trodden it; no mountain so far off that their eyes have not scanned its grandeur.

We took nearly a week in going to our hunting-grounds and out from them again. This was tedious work, for the pace was slow, and it was accompanied with some real labor. In places the mountain paths were very steep and the ponies could with difficulty scramble

THE INDIANS WE MET.

68

where, many years before, some fur-trapper had chopped a deeper blaze than usual in making out a "spotted line" — man's first highway in the primeval forest; or on some hill-side we would come across the more recent, but already half-obliterated, traces of a miner's handiwork. The trapper and the miner were the pioneers of the mountains, as the hunter and the cowboy have been the pioneers of the plains; they are all of the same type, these sinewy men of the border, fearless and self-reliant, who are forever driven restlessly onward through the wilderness by the half-formed desires that make their eyes haggard

along them; and once or twice they got falls that no animals less tough could have survived, Walla Walla being the unfortunate that suffered most. Often, moreover, we would come to a windfall, where the fallen trees lay heaped crosswise on one another in the wildest confusion, and a road had to be cleared by ax work. It was marvelous to see the philosophy with which the wise little beasts behaved, picking their way gingerly through these rough spots, hopping over fallen tree-trunks, or stepping between them in places where an Eastern horse would have snapped his leg short off, and walking composedly along

CARRYING FRESH MEAT TO CAMP.

narrow ledges with steep precipices below. They were tame and friendly, being turned loose at night, and not only staying near by, but also allowing themselves to be caught without difficulty in the morning; industriously gleaning the scant food to be found in the burnt places or along the edges of the brooks, and often in the evening standing in a patient, solemn semicircle round the camp fire, just beyond where we were seated. Walla Walla, the little mule, was always in scrapes. Once we spent a morning of awkward industry in washing our clothes; having finished, we spread the partially cleansed array upon the bushes and departed on a hunt. On returning, to our horror we spied the miserable Walla Walla shamefacedly shambling off from the neighborhood of the wash, having partly chewed up every individual garment and completely undone all our morning's labor.

At first we did not have good weather. The Indians, of whom we met a small band,— said to be Flatheads or their kin, on a visit from the coast region,— had set fire to the woods not far away, and the smoke became so dense as to hurt our eyes, to hide the sun at midday, and to veil all objects from our sight as completely as if there had been a heavy fog. Then we had two days of incessant rain, which rendered our camp none too comfortable; but when this cleared we found it had put out the fire and settled all the smoke, leaving a brilliant sky overhead.

We first camped in a narrow valley, surrounded by mountains so tall that except at noonday it lay in the shadow; and it was only when we were out late on the higher foot-hills that we saw the sun sink in a flame behind the distant ranges. The trees grew tall and thick, the underbrush choking the ground between their trunks, and their branches inter-

little water wrens — the water-ousel of the books — made this brook their home. They were shaped like thrushes, and sometimes warbled sweetly, yet they lived right in the torrent, not only flitting along the banks and wading

STALKING GOATS.

lacing so that the sun's rays hardly came through them. There were very few open glades, and these were not more than a dozen rods or so across. Even on the mountains it was only when we got up very high indeed, or when we struck an occasional bare spur, or shoulder, that we could get a glimpse into the open. Elsewhere we could never see a hundred yards ahead of us, and like all plainsmen or mountaineers we at times felt smothered under the trees, and longed to be where we could look out far and wide on every side; we felt as if our heads were in hoods. A broad brook whirled and eddied past our camp, and a little below us was caught in a deep, narrow gorge, where the strangling rocks churned its swift current into spray and foam, and changed its murmurous humming and splashing into an angry roar. Strange

in the edges, but plunging boldly into mid-stream, and half walking, half flying along the bottom, deep under water, and perching on the slippery, spray-covered rocks of the waterfall or skimming over and through the rapids even more often than they ran along the margins of the deep, black pools.

White-tail deer were plentiful, and we kept our camp abundantly supplied with venison, varying it with all the grouse we wanted, and with quantities of fresh trout. But I myself spent most of my time after the quarry I had come to get — the white goat.

White goats have been known to hunters ever since Lewis and Clarke crossed the continent, but they have always ranked as the very rarest and most difficult to get of all American game. This reputation they owe to the nature of their haunts, rather than to their own wariness, for they have been so little disturbed that they are less shy than either deer or sheep. They are found here and there on the highest, most inaccessible mountain peaks down even to Arizona and New Mexico; but being fitted for cold climates, they are extremely scarce everywhere south of Montana and northern Idaho, and the great majority even of the most experienced hunters have hardly so much as heard of their existence. In Washington Territory, northern Idaho, and north-western Montana they are not uncommon, and are plentiful in parts of the mountain ranges of British America and Alaska. Their preference for the highest peaks is due mainly to their dislike of warmth, and in the north — even south of the Canadian line — they are found much lower down the mountains than is the case farther south. They are very conspicuous animals, with their snow-white coats and polished black horns, but their pursuit necessitates so much toil and hardship that not one in ten of the professional hunters has ever killed one; and I know of but one or two Eastern sportsmen who can boast a goat's head as a trophy. But this will soon cease to be the case; for the Canadian Pacific Railway has opened the haunts where the goats are most plentiful, and any moderately adventurous and hardy rifleman can be sure of getting one by taking a little time, and that, too, whether he is a skilled hunter or not, since at present the game is not difficult to approach. The white goat will be common long after the elk has vanished, and it has already outlasted the buffalo. Few sportsmen henceforth — indeed, hardly any — will ever boast a buffalo head of their own killing; but the number of riflemen who can place to their credit the prized white fleeces and jet-black horns will steadily increase.

The Missourian, during his career as a Rocky Mountain hunter, had killed five white goats. The first he had shot near Canyon City, Colorado, and never having heard of any such animal before had concluded afterward that it was one of a flock of recently imported Angora goats, and accordingly, to avoid trouble, buried it where it lay; and it was not until fourteen years later, when he came up to the Cœur d'Alêne and shot another, that he became aware what he had killed. He described them as being bold, pugnacious animals, not easily startled, and extremely tenacious of life. Once he had set a large hound at one which he came across while descending an ice-swollen river in early spring. The goat made no attempt to flee or to avoid the hound, but coolly awaited its approach and killed it with one wicked thrust of the horns; for the latter are as sharp as needles, and are used for

stabbing, not butting. Another time he caught a goat in a bear trap set on a game trail. Its leg was broken, and he had to pack it out on pony-back, a two-days' journey, to the settlement; yet in spite of such rough treatment it lived a week after it got there, when, unfortunately, the wounded leg mortified. It fought most determinedly, but soon became reconciled to captivity, eating with avidity all the grass it was given, recognizing its keeper, and grunting whenever he brought it food or started to walk away before it had had all it wished. The goats he had shot lived in ground where the walking was tiresome to the last degree, and where it was almost impossible not to make a good deal of noise; and nothing but their boldness and curiosity enabled him ever to kill any. One he shot while waiting at a pass for deer. The goat, an old male, came up, and fairly refused to leave the spot, walking round in the underbrush and finally mounting a great fallen log, where he staid snorting and stamping angrily until the Missourian lost patience and killed him.

For three or four days I hunted steadily and without success, and it was as hard work as any I had ever undertaken. Both Merrifield and I were accustomed to a life in the saddle,

DOWN BRAKES!

and although we had varied it with an occasional long walk after deer or sheep, yet we were utterly unable to cope with the Missourian when it came to mountaineering. When we had previously hunted, in the Big Horn mountains, we had found stout moccasins most comfortable, and extremely useful for still-hunting through the great woods and among the open glades; but the multitudinous sharp rocks and sheer, cliff-like slopes of the Cœur

71

THE FIRST SHOT.

evergreen forest, except where an occasional cliff jutted out, or where there were great landslides, each perhaps half a mile long and a couple of hundred yards across, covered with loose slates or granite bowlders.

We always went above the domain of the deer, and indeed saw few evidences of life. Once or twice we came to the round footprints of cougars, which are said to be great enemies of the goats, but we never caught a glimpse of the sly beasts themselves. Another time I shot a sable from a spruce, up which the little fox-headed animal had rushed with the agility of a squirrel. There were plenty of old tracks of bear and elk, but no new ones; and occasionally we saw the foot-marks of the great timber wolf.

But the trails at which we looked with the most absorbed interest were those that showed the large, round hoof-marks of the white goats. They had worn deep paths to certain clay licks in the slides, which they must have visited often in the early spring, for the trails

d'Alêne rendered our moccasins absolutely useless, for the first day's tramp bruised our feet till they were sore and slit our foot-gear into ribbons, besides tearing our clothes. Merrifield was then crippled, having nothing else but his cowboy boots; fortunately, I had taken in addition a pair of shoes with soles thickly studded with nails.

We would start immediately after breakfast each morning, carrying a light lunch in our pockets, and go straight up the mountain sides for hours at a time, varying it by skirting the broad, terrace-like ledges, or by clambering along the cliff crests. The climbing was very hard. The slope was so steep that it was like going up stairs; now through loose earth, then through a shingle of pebbles or sand, then over rough rocks, and again over a layer of pine needles as smooth and slippery as glass, while brittle, dry sticks that snapped at a touch, and loose stones that rattled down if so much as brushed, strewed the ground everywhere, the climber stumbling and falling over them and finding it almost absolutely impossible to proceed without noise, unless at a rate of progress too slow to admit of getting anywhere. Often, too, we would encounter dense underbrush, perhaps a thicket of little burnt balsams, as prickly and brittle as so much coral; or else a heavy growth of laurel, all the branches pointing downward, and to be gotten through only by main force. Over all grew the vast

72

THE LAST SHOT

were little traveled when we were in the mountains during September. These clay licks were mere holes in the banks, and were in springtime visited by other animals besides goats; there were old deer trails to them. The clay seemed to contain something that both birds and beasts were fond of, for I frequently saw flocks of cross-bills light in the licks and stay there for many minutes at a time, scratching the smooth surface with their little claws and bills. The goat trails led away in every direction from the licks, but usually went up hill, zigzagging or in a straight line, and continually growing fainter as they went farther off, where the animals scattered to their feeding-grounds. In the spring-time the goats are clad with a dense coat of long white wool, and there were shreds and tufts of this on all the twigs of the bushes under which the paths passed; in the early fall the coat is shorter and less handsome.

Although these game paths were so deeply worn they yet showed very little fresh goat sign; in fact, we came across the recent trails of but two of the animals we were after. One of these we came quite close to, but never saw it, for we must have frightened it by the noise we made; it certainly, to judge by its tracks, which we followed for a long time, took itself straight out of the country. The other I finally got, after some heart-breaking work and a complicated series of faults committed and misfortunes endured.

I had been, as usual, walking and clambering over the mountains all day long, and in mid-afternoon reached a great slide, with half-way across it a tree. Under this I sat down to rest, my back to the trunk, and had been there but a few minutes when my companion, the Missourian, suddenly whispered to me that a goat was coming down the slide at its edge, near the woods. I was in a most uncomfortable position for a shot. Twisting my head round, I could see the goat waddling down-hill, looking just like a handsome tame billy, especially when at times he stood upon a stone to glance around, with all four feet close together. I cautiously tried to shift my position, and at once dislodged some pebbles, at the sound of which the goat sprang promptly up on the bank, his whole mien changing into one of alert, alarmed curiosity. He was less than a hundred yards off, so I risked a shot, all cramped and twisted though I was. But my bullet went low; I only broke his left fore leg, and he disappeared over the bank like a flash. We raced and scrambled after him, and the Missourian, an excellent tracker, took up the bloody trail. It went along the hill-side for nearly a mile, and then turned straight up the mountain, the Missourian leading with his long,

free gait, while I toiled after him at a dogged trot. The trail went up the sharpest and steepest places, skirting the cliffs and precipices. At one spot I nearly came to grief for good and all, for in running along a shelving ledge, covered with loose slates, one of these slipped as I stepped on it, throwing me clear over the brink. However, I caught in a pine top, bounced down through it, and brought up in a balsam with my rifle all right, and myself unhurt except for the shaking. I scrambled up at once and raced on after my companion, whose limbs and wind seemed alike incapable of giving out. This work lasted for a couple of hours.

The trail came into a regular game path and grew fresher, the goat having stopped to roll and wallow in the dust now and then. Suddenly, on the top of the mountain, we came upon him close up to us. He had just risen from rolling and stood behind a huge fallen log, his back barely showing above it as he turned his head to look at us. I was completely winded, and had lost my strength as well as my breath, while great beadlike drops of sweat stood in my eyes; but I steadied myself as well as I could and aimed to break the backbone, the only shot open to me, and not a difficult one at such a short distance. However, my bullet went just too high, cutting the skin right above the long spinal bones over the shoulders; and the speed with which that three-legged goat went down the precipitous side of the mountain would have done credit to an antelope on the level.

Weary and disgusted, we again took up the trail. It led straight down-hill, and we followed it at a smart pace. Down and down it went, into the valley and straight to the edge of the stream, but half a mile above camp. The goat had crossed the water on a fallen tree trunk, and we took the same path. Once across it had again gone right up the mountain. We followed it as fast as we could, although pretty nearly done out, until it was too dark to see the blood stains any longer, and then returned to camp, dispirited and so tired that we could hardly drag ourselves along, for we had been going at speed for five hours, up and down the roughest and steepest ground.

But we were confident the goat would not travel far with such a wound after he had been chased as we had chased him. Next morning at daybreak we again climbed the mountain and took up the trail. Soon it led into others and we lost it, but we kept up the hunt nevertheless for hour after hour, making continually wider and wider circles. At last, about midday, our perseverance was rewarded, for coming silently out on a great bare cliff shoulder, I spied the goat lying on a ledge below me and some seventy yards off. This time I shot true, and he rose only to fall back dead; and a minute afterward we were standing over him, handling the glossy black horns and admiring the snow-white coat.

After this we struck our tent and shifted camp some thirty miles to a wide valley through whose pine-clad bottom flowed a river, hurrying on to the Pacific between unending forests. On one hand the valley was hemmed in by an unbroken line of frowning cliffs, and on the other by chains of lofty mountains in whose sides the ravines cut deep gashes.

The clear weather had grown colder. At night the frost skimmed with thin ice the edges of the ponds and small lakes that at long intervals dotted the vast reaches of woodland. But we were very comfortable, and hardly needed our furs, for as evening fell we kindled huge fires, to give us both light and warmth; and even in very cold weather a man can sleep out comfortably enough with no bedding if he lights two fires and gets in between them, or finds a sheltered nook or corner across whose front a single great blaze can be made. The long walks and our work as cragsmen hardened our thews, and made us eat and sleep as even our life on the ranch could hardly do: the mountaineer must always be more sinewy than the horseman. The clear, cold water of the swift streams too was a welcome change from the tepid and muddy currents of the rivers of the plains; and we heartily enjoyed the baths, a plunge into one of the icy pools making us gasp for breath and causing the blood to tingle in our veins with the shock.

Our tent was pitched in a little glade, which was but a few yards across, and carpeted thickly with the red kinnikinic berries, in their season beloved of bears, and from the leaves of which bush Indians make a substitute for tobacco. Little three-toed woodpeckers with yellow crests scrambled about over the trees near by, while the great log-cocks hammered and rattled on the tall dead trunks. Jays that were all of dark blue came familiarly round camp in company with the ever-present moose-birds or whisky jacks. There were many grouse in the woods, of three kinds,— blue, spruce, and ruffed,— and these varied our diet and also furnished us with some sport with our rifles, as we always shot them in rivalry. That is, each would take a shot in turn, aiming at the head of the bird, as it perched motionless on the limb of a tree or stopped for a second while running along the ground; then if he missed or hit the bird anywhere but in the head, the other scored one and took the shot. The resulting tally was a good test of comparative

skill; and rivalry always tends to keep a man's shooting up to the mark.

Once or twice, when we had slain deer, we watched by the carcasses, hoping that they would attract a bear, or perhaps one of the huge timber wolves whose mournful, sinister howling we heard each night. But there were no bears in the valley; and the wolves, those cruel, crafty beasts, were far too cunning to come to the bait while we were there. We saw nothing but crowds of ravens, whose hoarse barking and croaking filled the air as they circled around overhead, lighted in the trees, or quarreled over the carcass. Yet although we saw no game it was very pleasant to sit out, on the still evenings, among the tall pines or on the edge of the great gorge, until the afterglow of the sunset was dispelled by the beams of the frosty moon. Now and again the hush would be suddenly broken by the long howling of a wolf, that echoed and rang under the hollow woods and through the deep chasms until they resounded again, while it made our hearts bound and the blood leap in our veins. Then there would be silence once more, broken only by the rush of the river and the low moaning and creaking of the pines; or the strange calling of the owls might be answered by the far-off, unearthly laughter of a loon, its voice carried through the stillness a marvelous distance from the little lake on which it was swimming.

One day, after much toilsome and in places almost dangerous work, we climbed to the very top of the nearest mountain chain, and from it looked out over a limitless, billowy field of snow-capped ranges. Up above the timber line were snow-grouse and huge, hoary-white woodchucks, but no trace of the game we were after; for, rather to our surprise, the few goat signs we saw were in the timber. I did not catch another glimpse of the animals themselves until my holiday was almost over and we were preparing to break camp. Then I saw two. I had spent a most laborious day on the mountain as usual, following the goat paths, which were well-trodden trails leading up the most inaccessible places; certainly the white goats are marvelous climbers, doing it all by main strength and perfect command over their muscles, for they are heavy, clumsy seeming animals, the reverse of graceful, and utterly without any look of light agility. As usual, towards evening I was pretty well tired out, for it would be difficult to imagine harder work than to clamber unendingly up and down the huge cliffs. I came down along a great jutting spur, broken by a series of precipices, with flat terraces at their feet, the terraces being covered with trees and bushes, and running, with many breaks and interruptions, parallel to each other across the face of the mountains. On one of these terraces was a space of hard clay ground beaten perfectly bare of vegetation by the hoofs of the goats, with, in the middle, a hole, two or three feet in width, that was evidently in the spring used as a lick. Most of the tracks were old, but there was one trail coming diagonally down the side of the mountain on which there were two or three that were very fresh. It was getting late, so I did not stay long, but continued the descent. The terrace on which the lick was situated lay but a few hundred yards above the valley, and then came a level, marshy plain a quarter of a mile broad, between the base of the mountain and the woods. Leading down to this plain was another old goat-trail, which went to a small, boggy pool, which the goats must certainly have often visited in the spring; but it was then unused.

When I reached the farther side of the plain and was about entering the woods, I turned to look over the mountain once more, and my eye was immediately caught by two white objects that were moving along the terrace, about half a mile to one side of the lick. That they were goats was evident at a glance, their white bodies contrasting sharply with the green vegetation. They came along very rapidly, giving me no time to get back over the plain, and stopped for a short time at the lick, right in sight from where I was, although too far off for me to tell anything about their size. I think they smelt my foot-prints in the soil; at any rate they were very watchful, one of them always jumping up on a rock or fallen log to mount guard when the other halted to browse. The sun had just set; it was impossible to advance across the open plain, which they scanned at every glance; and to skirt it and climb up any other place than the pass down which I had come — itself a goat-trail — would have taken till long after nightfall. All I could do was to stay where I was and watch them, until in the dark I slipped off unobserved and made the best of my way to camp, resolved to hunt them up on the morrow.

Shortly after noon next day we were at the terrace, having approached with the greatest caution, and only after a minute examination, with the field-glasses, of all the neighboring mountain. I wore moccasins, so as to make no noise. We soon found that one of the trails was evidently regularly traveled, probably every evening, and we determined to lie in wait by it, so as either to catch the animals as they came down to feed, or else to mark them if they got out on some open spot on the terraces where they could be stalked. As an ambush we chose a ledge in the cliff below a terrace, with, in front, a breastwork of the natural rock some five feet high. It was perhaps fifty yards from the trail. I hid myself on this ledge, having arranged on the rock breastwork a few pine branches, through which to fire, and waited, hour after hour, continually scanning the mountain carefully with the glasses. There was very little life. Occasionally a chickaree or chipmunk scurried out from among the trunks of the great pines to pick up the cones which he had previously bitten off from the upper branches; a noisy Clarke's crow clung for some time in the top of a hemlock; and occasionally flocks of cross-bill went by, with swift undulating flight and low calls. From time to time I peeped cautiously over the pine branches on the breastwork; and the last time I did this I suddenly saw two goats, that had come noiselessly down, standing motionless directly opposite to me, their suspicions evidently aroused by something. I gently shoved the rifle over one of the boughs; the largest goat turned its head sharply round to look, as it stood quartering to me, and the bullet went fairly through the lungs. Both animals promptly ran off along the terrace, and I raced after them in my moccasins, skirting the edge of the cliff, where there were no trees or bushes. As I made no noise and could run very swiftly on the bare cliff edge, I succeeded in coming out into the first little glade, or break, in the terrace at the same time that the goats did. The first to come out of the bushes was the big one I had shot at, an old she, as it turned out; while the other, a yearling ram, followed. The big one turned to look at me, as she mounted a fallen tree that lay across a chasm-like rent in the terrace; the light red frothy blood covered her muzzle, and I paid no further heed to her as she slowly walked along the log, but bent my attention towards the yearling, that was galloping and scrambling up an almost perpendicular path that led across the face of the cliff above. Holding my rifle just over it, I fired, breaking its neck, and it rolled down some fifty or sixty yards, almost to where I stood. I then went after the old goat, which had lain down; as I approached she feebly tried to rise and show fight, but her strength was spent, her blood had ebbed away, and she fell back lifeless in the effort. They were both good specimens, the old one being unusually large, with fine horns. White goats are squat, heavy beasts; not so tall as black-tail deer, but weighing more.

Early next morning I came back with my two men to where the goats were lying, taking along the camera. Having taken their photographs and skinned them we went back to camp, hunted up the ponies and mules, who had been shifting for themselves during the past few days, packed up our tent, trophies, and other belongings, and set off for the settlements, well pleased with our trip.

I suppose the sport to be had among the tremendous mountain masses of the Himalayas must stand above all other kinds of hill shooting; yet after all it is hard to believe that it can yield much more pleasure than that felt by the American hunter when he follows the lordly elk and the grizzly among the timbered slopes of the Rockies, or the big-horn and the white-fleeced, jet-horned antelope goat over their towering and barren peaks.

Theodore Roosevelt.

76

CHAPTER SIX

FRONTIER TYPES

THE old race of Rocky Mountain hunters and trappers, of reckless, dauntless Indian fighters, is now fast dying out. Yet here and there these restless wanderers of the untrodden wilderness still linger, in wooded fastnesses so inaccessible that the miners have not yet explored them, in mountain valleys so far off that no ranchman has yet driven his herds thither. To this day many of them wear the fringed tunic or hunting-shirt, made of buckskin, or homespun, and belted in at the waist — the most picturesque and distinctively national dress ever worn in America. It was the dress in which Daniel Boone was clad when he first passed through the trackless forests of the Alleghanies and penetrated into the heart of Kentucky, to enjoy such hunting as no man of his race had ever had before; it was the dress worn by grim old Davy Crocket when he fell at the Alamo. The wild soldiery of the backwoods wore it when they marched to victory over Ferguson and Pakenham, at King's Mountain and New Orleans; when they conquered the French towns of the Illinois; and when they won at the cost of Red Eagle's warriors the bloody triumph of the Horseshoe Bend.

These old-time hunters have been the forerunners of the white advance throughout all our Western land. Soon after the beginning of the present century they boldly struck out beyond the Mississippi, steered their way across the flat and endless seas of grass, or pushed up the valleys of the great lonely rivers, crossed the passes that wound among the towering peaks of the Rockies, toiled over the melancholy wastes of sage brush and alkali, and at last, breaking through the gloomy woodland that belts the coast, looked out on the heaving waves of the greatest of all the oceans. They lived for months, often for years, among the Indians, now as friends, now as foes, warring, hunting, and marrying with them; they acted as guides for exploring parties, as scouts for the soldiers who from time to time were sent against the different hostile tribes. At long intervals they came into some frontier settlement or some fur company's fort, posted in the heart of the wilderness, to dispose of their bales of furs, or to replenish their stock of ammunition and purchase a scanty supply of coarse food and clothing.

From that day to this they have not changed their way of life. But there are not many of them left now. The basin of the Upper Missouri was their last stronghold, being the last great hunting-ground of the Indians, with whom the white trappers were always fighting and bickering, but who nevertheless by their presence protected the game that gave the trappers their livelihood. My cattle were among the very first to come into the land, at a time when the buffalo and the beaver still abounded, and then the old hunters were common. Many a time I have hunted with them, spent the night in their smoky cabins, or had them as guests at my ranch. But in a couple of years after the inrush of the cattle-men the last herds of the buffalo were destroyed, and the beaver were trapped out of all the plains' streams. Then the hunters vanished likewise, save that here and there one or two still remain in some nook or out-of-the-way corner. The others wandered off restlessly over the land — some to join their brethren in the Cœur d'Alêne or the northern Rockies, others to the coast ranges or to far-away Alaska. Moreover, their ranks were soon thinned by death, and the places of the dead were no longer taken by new recruits. They led hard lives, and the unending strain of their toilsome and dangerous existence shattered even such iron frames as theirs. They were killed in drunken brawls, or in nameless fights with roving Indians; they died by one of the thousand accidents incident to the business of their lives — by flood or quicksand, by cold or starvation, by the stumble of a horse or a foot-slip on the edge of a cliff; they perished by diseases brought on by terrible privation and aggravated by the savage orgies with which it was varied.

Yet there was not only much that was attractive in their wild, free, reckless lives, but there was also very much good about the men themselves. They were — and such of them as are left still are — frank, bold, and self-reliant to a degree. They fear neither man, brute, nor element. They are generous and hospitable; they stand loyally by their friends, and pursue their enemies with bitter and vindictive hatred. For the rest, they differ among themselves in their good and bad points even more markedly than do men in civilized life, for out on the border virtue and wickedness alike take on very pronounced colors. A man who in civilization would be merely a back-biter becomes a murderer on the frontier; and, on the other hand, he who in the city would do nothing more than bid you a cheery good-morning shares his last bit of sun-jerked venison with you when both are threatened by starvation in the wilderness. One hunter may be a dark-browed, evil-eyed ruffian, ready to kill cattle or run off horses without hesitation, who if game fails will at once, in Western phrase, "take to the road" — that is, become a highwayman. The next is perhaps a quiet, kindly, simple-hearted man, law-abiding, modestly unconscious of the worth of his own fearless courage and iron endurance, always faithful to his friends, and full of chivalric and tender loyalty to women.

The hunter is the arch-type of freedom. His well-being rests in no man's hands save his own. He chops down and hews out the logs for his hut, or perhaps makes merely a rude dug-out in the side of a hill, with a skin roof, or skin flaps for the door. He buys a little flour and salt, and in times of plenty also sugar and tea; but not much, for it must all be carried hundreds of miles on the backs of his shaggy pack-ponies. In one corner of the hut, a bunk covered with deer-skins forms his bed; a kettle and a frying-pan may be all his cooking-utensils. When he can get no fresh meat he falls back on his stock of jerked venison, dried in long strips over the fire or in the sun.

Most of the trappers are Americans, but there are some Frenchmen and half-breeds among them. Both of the last, if on the plains, occasionally make use of queer wooden carts, very rude in shape, with stout wheels that make a most doleful squeaking. In old times they all had Indian wives; but nowadays those who live among and intermarry with the Indians are looked down upon by the other frontiersmen, who contemptuously term them "squaw-men." All of them depend upon their rifles only for food and for self-defense, and make their living by trapping, peltries being very valuable and yet not bulky. They are good game shots, especially the pure Americans; although, of course, they are very boast-ful, and generally stretch the truth tremendously in telling about their own marksmanship. Still they often do very remarkable shooting, both for speed and accuracy. One of their feats, that I never could learn to copy, is to make excellent shooting after nightfall. Of course all this applies only to the regular hunters; not to the numerous pretenders who hang around the outskirts of the towns to try to persuade unwary strangers to take them for guides.

On one of my trips to the mountains I happened to come across several old-style hunters at the same time. Two were on their way out of the woods, after having been all winter and spring without seeing a white face. They had been lucky, and their battered pack-saddles carried bales of valuable furs — fisher, sable, otter, mink, beaver. The two men, though fast friends and allies for many years, contrasted oddly. One was a short, square-built, good-humored Kanuck, always laughing and talking, who interlarded his conversation with a singularly original mixture of the most villainous French and English profanity. His partner was an American, gray-eyed, tall and straight as a young pine, with a saturnine, rather haughty face, and proud bearing. He spoke very little, and then in low tones, never using an oath; but he showed now and then a most unexpected sense of dry humor. Both were marvels of bronzed and rugged strength. Neither had the slightest touch of the bully in his nature; they treated others with the respect that they exacted for themselves. They bore an excellent reputation as being not only highly skilled in woodcraft and the use of the rifle, but also men of tried courage and strict integrity, whose word could be always implicitly trusted.

I had with me at the time a hunter who, though their equal as marksman or woodsman, was their exact opposite morally. He was a pleasant companion and useful assistant, being very hard-working, and possessing a temper that never was ruffled by anything. He was also a good-looking fellow, with honest brown eyes; but he no more knew the difference between right and wrong than did Adam before the fall. Had he been at all conscious of his wickedness, or had he possessed the least sense of shame, he would have been unbearable as a companion; but he was so perfectly pleasant and easy, so good-humoredly tolerant of virtue in others, and he so wholly lacked even a glimmering suspicion that murder, theft, and adultery were matters of anything more than individual taste, that I actually grew to be rather fond of him. He never related any of his past deeds of wickedness as matters either for boastfulness or for

A FUGITIVE.

79

A FRENCH-CANADIAN TRAPPER.

a gun] and begun shooting; but I hit him first, and away he rode. I started to get on my horse to follow him; but there was a little Irishman there who said he'd never killed a man, and he begged hard for me to give him my gun and let him go after the other man and finish him. So I let him go; and when he caught up, blamed if the little cuss did n't get so nervous that he fired off into the ground, and the darned bullet struck a crowbar, and glanced up, and hit the other man square in the head and killed him! Now, that *was* a funny shot, was n't it?"

The fourth member of our party round the camp-fire that night was a powerfully built trapper, partly French by blood, who wore a gayly colored capote, or blanket-coat, a greasy fur cap, and moccasins. He had grizzled hair, and a certain uneasy, half-furtive look about the eyes. Once or twice he showed a curious reluctance about allowing a man to approach him suddenly from behind. Altogether his actions were so odd that I felt some curiosity to learn his history. It turned out that he had been through a rather uncanny experience the winter before. He and another man had gone into a remote basin, or inclosed valley, in the heart of the mountains, where game

regret; they were simply narrated incidentally in the course of conversation. Thus once, in speaking of the profits of his different enterprises, he casually mentioned making a good deal of money as a Government scout in the South-west by buying cartridges from some negro troops at a cent apiece and selling them to the hostile Apaches for a dollar each. His conduct was not due to sympathy with the Indians, for it appeared that later on he had taken part in massacring some of these same Apaches when they were prisoners. He brushed aside as irrelevant one or two questions which I put to him: matters of sentiment were not to be mixed up with a purely mercantile speculation. Another time we were talking of the curious angles at which bullets sometimes fly off when they ricochet. To illustrate the matter he related an experience which I shall try to give in his own words:

"One time, when I was keeping a saloon down in New Mexico, there was a man owed me a grudge. Well, he took sick of the small-pox, and the doctor told him he'd sure die, and he said if that was so he reckoned he'd kill me first. So he come a-riding in with his gun [in the West a revolver is generally called

was very plentiful; indeed, it was so abundant that they decided to pass the winter there. Accordingly they put up a log-cabin, working hard, and merely killing enough meat for their immediate use. Just as it was finished winter set in with tremendous snow-storms. Going out to hunt, in the first lull, they found, to their consternation, that every head of game had left the valley. Not an animal was to be found therein; they had abandoned it for their winter haunts. The outlook for the two adventurers was appalling. They were afraid of trying to break out through the deep snow-drifts, and starvation stared them in the face if they staid. The man that I met had his dog with him. They put themselves on very short commons, so as to use up their flour as slowly as possible, and hunted unweariedly, but saw nothing. Soon a violent quarrel broke out between them. The other man, a fierce, sullen fellow, insisted that the dog should be killed, but the owner was exceedingly attached to it, and refused. For a couple of weeks they spoke no word to each other, though cooped in the little narrow pen of logs. Then one night the owner of the dog was wakened by the animal crying out; the other man had tried to kill it with his knife, but failed. The provisions were now almost exhausted, and the two men were glaring at each other with the rage of maddened, ravening hunger. Neither dared to sleep, for fear that the other would kill him. Then the one who owned the dog at last spoke, and proposed that, to give each a chance for his life, they should separate. He would take half of the handful of flour that was left and start off to try to get home; the other should stay where he was; and if he tried to follow the first, he was warned that he would be shot without mercy. A like fate was to be the portion of the wanderer if driven to return to the hut. The arrangement was agreed to and the two men separated, neither daring to turn his back while they were within rifle-shot of each other. For two days the one who went off toiled on with weary weakness through the snow-drifts. Late on the second afternoon, as he looked back from a high ridge, he saw in the far distance a black speck against the snow, coming along on his trail. His companion was dogging his footsteps. Immediately he followed his own trail back a little and lay in ambush. At dusk his companion came stealthily up, rifle in hand, peering cautiously ahead, his drawn face showing the starved, eager ferocity of a wild beast, and the man he was hunting shot him down exactly as if he had been one. Leaving the body where it fell, the wanderer continued his journey, the dog staggering painfully behind him. The next evening he baked his last cake and divided it with the dog. In the morning, with his belt drawn still tighter round his skeleton body, he once more set out, with apparently only a few hours of dull misery between him and death. At noon he crossed the track of a huge timber-wolf; instantly the dog gave tongue, and, rallying its strength, ran along the trail. The man struggled after. At last his strength gave out and he sat down to die; but while sitting still, slowly stiffening with the cold, he heard the dog baying in the woods. Shaking off his mortal numbness, he crawled towards the sound, and found the wolf over the body of a deer that he had just killed, and keeping the dog from it. At the approach of the new assailant the wolf sullenly drew off, and man and dog tore the raw deer-flesh with hideous eagerness. It made them very sick for the next twenty-four hours; but, lying by the carcass for two or three days, they recovered strength. A week afterwards the trapper reached a miner's cabin in safety. There he told his tale, and the unknown man who alone might possibly have contradicted it lay dead in the depths of the wolf-haunted forest.

The cowboys, who have supplanted these old hunters and trappers as the typical men of the plains, themselves lead lives that are almost as full of hardship and adventure. The unbearable cold of winter sometimes makes the small outlying camps fairly uninhabitable if fuel runs short; and if the line-riders are caught in a blizzard while making their way to the home ranch, they are lucky if they get off with nothing worse than frozen feet and faces.

They are, in the main, hard-working, faithful fellows, but of course are frequently obliged to get into scrapes through no fault of their own. Once, while out on a wagon trip, I got caught while camped by a spring on the prairie, through my horses all straying. A few miles off was the camp of two cowboys, who were riding the line for a great Southern cow-outfit. I did not even know their names, but happening to pass by them I told of my loss, and the day after they turned up with the missing horses, which they had been hunting for twenty-four hours. All I could do in return was to give them some reading-matter — something for which the men in these lonely camps are always grateful. Afterwards I spent a day or two with my new friends, and we became quite intimate. They were Texans. Both were quiet, clean-cut, pleasant-spoken young fellows, who did not even swear, except

81

THE OLD TRAPPER.

DISSOLUTE COW-PUNCHERS.

under great provocation; — and there can be no greater provocation than is given by a " mean " horse or a refractory steer. Yet, to my surprise, I found that they were, in a certain sense, fugitives from justice. They were complaining of the extreme severity of the winter weather, and mentioned their longing to go back to the South. The reason they could not was that the summer before they had taken part in a small civil war in one of the wilder counties of New Mexico. It had originated in a quarrel between two great ranches over their respective water rights and range rights — a quarrel of a kind rife among pastoral peoples since the days when the herdsmen of Lot and Abraham strove together for the grazing lands round the mouth of the Jordan. There were collisions between bands of armed cowboys, the cattle were harried from the springs, outlying camps were burned down, and the sons of the rival owners fought each other to the death with bowie-knife and revolver when they met at the drinking-booths of the squalid towns. Soon the smoldering jealousy which is ever existent between the Americans and Mexicans of the frontier was aroused, and when the original cause of quarrel was adjusted, a fierce race struggle took its place. It was soon quelled by the arrival of a sheriff's strong posse and the threat of interference by the regular troops, but not until after a couple of affrays, each attended with bloodshed. In one of these the American cowboys of a certain range, after a brisk fight, drove out the Mexican *vaqueros* from among them. In the other, to avenge the murder of one of their number, the cowboys gathered from the country round about and fairly stormed the " Greaser "— that is, Mexican — village where the murder had been committed, killing four of the inhabitants. My two friends had borne a part in this last affair. They were careful to give a rather cloudy account of the details, but I gathered that one of them was " wanted " as a participant, and the other as a witness.

However, they were both good fellows, and probably their conduct was justifiable, at least according to the rather fitful lights of the border. While sitting up late with them, around the sputtering fire, they became quite confidential. At first our conversation touched only the usual monotonous round of subjects worn threadbare in every cow-camp. A bunch of steers had been seen traveling over the scoria buttes to the head of Elk Creek; they were mostly Texan *doughgies,*— a name I have never seen written; it applies to young immigrant cattle,— but there were some of the Hash-Knife four-year-olds among them. A stray horse with a blurred brand on the left hip had just joined the bunch of saddle-ponies. The red F. V. cow, one of whose legs had been badly bitten by a wolf, had got mired down in an alkali spring, and when hauled out had charged upon her rescuer so viciously that he barely escaped. Sawback, the old mule, was getting over the effects of the rattlesnake bite. The river was going down, but the fords were still bad, and the quicksand at the Custer Trail crossing had worked along so that wagons had to be taken over opposite the blasted cotton-wood. One of the men had seen a Three-Seven-B rider who had just left the Green River round-up, and who brought news that they had found some cattle on the reservation, and were now holding about twelve hundred head

on the big brushy bottom below Rainy Butte. Bronco Jim, our local flash rider, had tried to ride the big bald-faced sorrel belonging to the Oregon horse-outfit, and had been bucked off and his face smashed in. This piece of information of course drew forth much condemnation of the unfortunate Jim's equestrian skill. It was at once agreed that he "was n't the sure-enough bronco-buster he thought himself," and he was compared very unfavorably to various heroes of the quirt and spurs who lived in Texas and Colorado; for the best rider, like the best hunter, is invariably either dead or else a resident of some other district.

These topics having been exhausted, we discussed the rumor that the vigilantes had given notice to quit to two men who had just built a shack at the head of the Little Dry, and whose horses included a suspiciously large number of different brands, most of them blurred. Then our conversation became more personal, and they asked if I would take some letters to post for them. Of course I said yes, and two letters — evidently the product of severe manual labor — were produced. Each was directed to a girl; and my companions, now very friendly, told me that they both had sweethearts, and for the next hour I listened to a full account of their charms and virtues.

But it is not often that plainsmen talk so easily. They are rather reserved, especially

A FIGHT IN THE STREET.

83

"DANCE HIGHER — DANCE FASTER."

lectual power. The gambler, with hawk eyes and lissom fingers, is scarcely classed as a criminal; indeed, he may be a very public-spirited citizen. But as his trade is so often plied in saloons,— and even if, as sometimes happens, he does not cheat, many of his opponents are certain to attempt to do so,— he is of necessity obliged to be skillful and ready with his weapon, and gambling rows are very common. Cowboys lose much of their money to gamblers; it is with them hard come and light go, for they exchange the wages of six months' grinding toil and lonely peril for three days' whooping carousal, spending their money on poisonous whisky or losing it over greasy cards in the vile dance houses. As already explained, they are in the main good men; and the disturbance that they cause in a town is done from sheer rough lightheartedness. They shoot off boot-heels or tall hats occasionally, or make some obnoxious butt "dance" by shooting round his feet; but they rarely meddle in this way with men who have not themselves played the fool. A fight in the streets is almost always a duel between two men who bear each other malice; it is only in a general mêlée in a saloon that outsiders often get hurt, and then it is their own fault, for they have no business to be there. One evening at Medora a cowboy spurred his horse up the steps of a rickety "hotel" piazza into the bar-room, where he began firing at the clock, the decanters, etc., the bartender meanwhile taking one shot at him, which missed. When he had emptied his revolver he threw down a roll of bank-notes on the counter, to pay for the damage that he had done, and galloped his horse out through the door, disappearing in the darkness with loud yells to a rattling accompaniment of pistol-shots interchanged between himself and some passer-by, who apparently began firing out of pure desire to enter into the spirit of the occasion — for it was the night of the Fourth of July, and all the country round about had come into town for a spree.

All this is mere horse-play; it is the cowboy's method of "painting the town red," as an interlude in his harsh, monotonous life. Of course there are plenty of hard characters among cowboys, but no more than among lumbermen and the like; only the cowboys

to strangers; and are certain to look with dislike on any man who, when they first meet him, talks a great deal. It is always a good plan, if visiting a strange camp or ranch, to be as silent as possible.

Another time, at a ranch not far from my own, I found among the cowboys gathered for the round-up two Bible-reading Methodists, who fearlessly lived up to their faith but did not obtrude their opinions on any one else, and were first-class workers, so that they had no trouble with the other men. Associated with them were two or three blear-eyed, slit-mouthed ruffians, who were as loose of tongue as of life.

Generally some form of stable government is provided for the counties as soon as their population has become at all fixed, the frontiersmen showing their national aptitude for organization. Then lawlessness is put down pretty effectively. For example, as soon as we organized the government of Medora — an excessively unattractive little hamlet, the county-seat of our huge, scantily settled county — we elected some good officers, built a log jail, prohibited all shooting in the streets, and enforced the prohibition, etc.

Up to that time there had been a good deal of lawlessness of one kind or another, only checked by an occasional piece of individual retribution or by a sporadic outburst of vigilance committee work. In such a society the desperadoes of every grade flourish. Many are merely ordinary rogues and swindlers, who rob and cheat on occasion, but are dangerous only when led by some villain of real intel-are so ready with their weapons that a bully in one of their camps is apt to be a murderer instead of merely a bruiser. Often, moreover, on a long trail, or in a far-off camp, where the men are for many months alone, feuds spring up that are in the end sure to be slaked in blood. As a rule, however, cowboys who become desperadoes soon perforce drop their original business, and are no longer employed on ranches, unless in counties or territories where there is very little heed paid to the law, and where, in consequence, a cattle-owner needs a certain number of hired bravos. Until within two or three years this was the case in parts of Arizona and New Mexico, where land claims were "jumped" and cattle stolen all the while, one effect being to insure high wages to every individual who combined murderous proclivities with skill in the use of the six-shooter.

Even in much more quiet regions different outfits vary greatly as regards the character of their employees: I know one or two where the men are good ropers and riders, but a gambling, brawling, hard-drinking set, always shooting each other or strangers. Generally, in such a case, the boss is himself as objectionable as his men; he is one of those who have risen by unblushing rascality, and is always sharply watched by his neighbors, because he is sure to try to shift calves on to his own cows, to brand any blurred animal with his own mark, and perhaps to attempt the alteration of perfectly plain brands. The last operation, however, has become very risky since the organization of the cattle country and the appointment of trained brand-readers as inspectors. These inspectors examine the hide of every animal slain, sold, or driven off, and it is wonderful to see how quickly they will detect signs of a brand having been tampered with. Now there is, in consequence, very little of this kind of dishonesty; whereas formerly herds were occasionally stolen almost bodily.

Claim-jumpers are, as a rule, merely blackmailers. Sometimes they will by threats drive an ignorant foreigner from his claim, but never an old frontiersman. They delight to squat down beside ranchmen who are themselves trying to keep land to which they are not entitled, and who therefore know that their only hope is to bribe or to bully the intruder.

Cattle-thieves, for the reason given above, are not common, although there are plenty of vicious, shiftless men who will kill a cow or a steer for the meat in winter, if they get a chance.

Horse-thieves, however, are always numerous and formidable on the frontier; though in our own country they have been summarily thinned out of late years. It is the fashion to laugh at the severity with which horse-stealing is punished on the border, but the reasons are evident. Horses are the most valuable property of the frontiersman, whether cowboy, hunter, or settler, and are often absolutely essential to his well-being, and even to his life. They are always marketable, and are very easily stolen, for they carry themselves off, instead of having to be carried. Horse-stealing is thus a most tempting business, especially

THE MAGIC OF THE "DROP."

85

to the more reckless ruffians, and it is always followed by armed men; and they can only be kept in check by ruthless severity. Frequently they band together with the road agents (highwaymen) and other desperadoes into secret organizations, which control and terrorize a district until overthrown by force. After the civil war a great many guerrillas, notably from Arkansas and Missouri, went out to the plains, often drifting northward. They took naturally to horse-stealing and kindred pursuits. Since I have been in the northern cattle country I have known of half a dozen former members of Quantrell's gang being hanged or shot.

The professional man-killers, or "bad men," may be horse-thieves or highwaymen, but more often are neither one nor the other. Some of them, like some of the Texan cowboys, become very expert in the use of the revolver, their invariable standby; but in the open a cool man with a rifle is always an overmatch for one of them, unless at very close quarters, on account of the superiority of his weapon. Some of the "bad men" are quiet, good fellows, who have been driven into their career by accident. One of them has perhaps at some time killed a man in self-defense; he acquires some reputation, and the neighboring

FROM LIFE.

bullies get to look on him as a rival whom it would be an honor to slay; so that from that time on he must be ever on the watch, must learn to draw quick and shoot straight,—the former being even more important than the latter,—and probably has to take life after life in order to save his own.

Some of these men are brave only because of their confidence in their own skill and strength; once convince them that they are overmatched and they turn into abject cowards. Others have nerves of steel and will face any odds, or certain death itself, without flinching a hand-breadth. I was once staying in a town where a desperately plucky fight took place. A noted desperado, an Arkansas man, had become involved in a quarrel with two others of the same kind, both Irishmen and partners. For several days all three lurked about the saloon-infested streets of the roaring little board-and-canvas "city," each trying to get "the drop,"—that is, the first shot,—the other inhabitants looking forward to the fight with pleased curiosity, no one dreaming of interfering. At last one of the partners got a chance at his opponent as the latter was walking into a gambling-hell, and broke his back near the hips; yet the crippled, mortally wounded man twisted around as he fell and

86

WHICH IS THE BAD MAN?

shot his slayer dead. Then, knowing that he had but a few moments to live, and expecting that his other foe would run up on hearing the shooting, he dragged himself by his arms out into the street. Immediately afterwards, as he anticipated, the second partner appeared, and was killed on the spot. The victor did not live twenty minutes. As in most of these encounters, all of the men who were killed deserved their fate. In my own not very extensive experience I can recall but one man killed in these fights whose death was regretted, and he was slain by a European. Generally every one is heartily glad to hear of the death of either of the contestants, and the only regret is that the other survives.

One curious shooting scrape that took place in Medora was worthy of being chronicled by Bret Harte. It occurred in the summer of 1884, I believe, but it may have been the year following. I did not see the actual occurrence, but I saw both men immediately afterwards; and I heard the shooting, which took place in a saloon on the bank, while I was swimming my horse across the river, holding my rifle up so as not to wet it. I will not give their full names, as I am not certain what has become of them; though I was told that one had since been either put in jail or hanged, I forget which. One of them was a saloon-keeper, familiarly called Welshy. The other man, Hay, had been bickering with him for some time. One day Hay, who had been defeated in a wrestling match by one of my own boys, and was out of temper, entered the other's saloon and became very abusive. The quarrel grew more and more violent, and suddenly Welshy whipped out his revolver and blazed away at Hay. The latter staggered slightly, shook himself, stretched out his hand, and *gave back to his would-be slayer the ball*, saying, "Here, man, here 's the bullet." It had glanced along his breast-bone, gone into the body, and come out at the point of the shoulder, when, being spent, it dropped down the sleeve into his hand. Next day the local paper, which rejoiced in the title of "The Bad Lands Cowboy," chronicled the event in the usual vague way as an "unfortunate occurrence" between "two of our most esteemed fellow-citizens." The editor was a good fellow, a college graduate, and a first-class base-ball player, who always stood up stoutly against any corrupt dealing; but, like all other editors in small Western towns, he was intimate with both combatants in almost every fight.

The winter after this occurrence I was away, and on my return began asking my foreman — a particular crony of mine — about the fates of my various friends. Among others I inquired after a traveling preacher who had come to our neighborhood — a good man, but irascible. After a moment's pause a gleam of remembrance came into my informant's eye: "Oh, the parson! Well — he beat a man over the head with an ax, and they put him in jail!" It certainly seemed a rather summary method of repressing a refractory parishioner. Another acquaintance had shared a like doom. "He started to go out of the country, but they ketched him at Bismarck and put him in jail" — apparently on general principles, for I did not hear of his having committed any specific crime. My foreman sometimes developed his own theories of propriety. I remember his objecting strenuously to a proposal to lynch a certain French-Canadian who had lived in his own cabin, back from the river, ever since the whites came into the land, but who was suspected of being a horse-thief. His chief point against the proposal was, not that the man was innocent, but that "it did n't seem anyways right to hang a man who had been so long in the country."

Sometimes we had a comic row. There was one huge man from Missouri called "The Pike," who had been the keeper of a wood-yard for steamboats on the Upper Missouri. Like most of his class, he was a hard case; and, though pleasant enough when sober, always insisted on fighting when drunk. One day, when on a spree, he announced his intention of thrashing the entire population of Medora seriatim, and began to make his promise good with great vigor and praiseworthy impartiality. He was victorious over the first two or three eminent citizens whom he encountered, and then tackled a gentleman known as "Cold Turkey Bill." Under ordinary circumstances Cold Turkey, though an able-bodied man, was no match for The Pike; but the latter was still rather drunk, and moreover was wearied by his previous combats. So Cold Turkey got him down, lay on him, choked him by the throat with one hand, and began pounding his face with a triangular rock held in the other. To the onlookers the fate of the battle seemed decided; but Cold Turkey better appreciated the endurance of his adversary, and it soon appeared that he sympathized with the traditional hunter who, having caught a wildcat, earnestly besought a comrade to help him let it go. While still pounding vigorously he raised an agonized wail: "Help me off, fellows, for the Lord's sake; he 's tiring me out!" There was no resisting so plaintive an appeal, and the bystanders at once abandoned their attitude of neutrality for one of armed intervention.

I have always been treated with the utmost courtesy by all cowboys, whether on the round-up or in camp; and the few real desperadoes

87

that I have seen were also perfectly polite. Indeed, I never was shot at maliciously but once. This was on an occasion when I had to pass the night in a little frontier hotel where the bar-room occupied the whole lower floor, and was in consequence the place where every one, drunk or sober, had to sit. My assailant was neither a cowboy nor a *bonâ fide* "bad man," but a broad-hatted ruffian of cheap and commonplace type, who had for the moment terrorized the other men in the bar-room, these being mostly sheep-herders and small grangers. The fact that I wore glasses, together with my evident desire to avoid a fight, apparently gave him the impression — a mistaken one — that I would not resent an injury.

The first deadly affray that took place in our town, after the cattle-men came in and regular settlement began, was between a Scotchman and a Minnesota man, the latter being one of the small stockmen. Both had shooting records, and each was a man with a varied past. The Scotchman, a noted bully, was the more daring of the two, but he was much too hot-headed and overbearing to be a match for his gray-eyed, hard-featured foe. After a furious quarrel and threats of violence, the Scotchman mounted his horse, and, rifle in hand, rode to the door of the mud ranch, perched on the brink of the river-bluff, where the American lived, and was instantly shot down by the latter from behind a corner of the building.

Later on I once opened a cowboy ball with the wife of the victor in this contest, the husband himself dancing opposite. It was the lanciers, and he knew all the steps far better than I did. He could have danced a minuet very well with a little practice. The scene reminded one of the ball where Bret Harte's heroine "danced down the middle with the man who shot Sandy Magee."

But though there were plenty of men present each of whom had shot his luckless Sandy Magee, yet there was no Lily of Poverty Flat. There is an old and true border saying that "the frontier is hard on women and cattle." There are some striking exceptions; but, as a rule, the grinding toil and hardship of a life passed in the wilderness, or on its outskirts, drive the beauty and bloom from a woman's face long before her youth has left her. By the time she is a mother she is sinewy and angular, with thin, compressed lips and furrowed, sallow brow. But she has a hundred qualities that atone for the grace she lacks. She is a good mother, and a hard-working housewife, always putting things to rights, washing and cooking for her stalwart spouse and offspring. She is faithful to her husband, and, like the true American that she is, exacts

faithfulness in return. Peril cannot daunt her, nor hardship and poverty appall her. Whether on the mountains in a log hut chinked with moss, in a sod or adobe hovel on the desolate prairie, or in a mere temporary camp, where the white-topped wagons have been drawn up in a protection-giving circle near some spring, she is equally at home. Clad in a dingy gown and a hideous sun-bonnet, she goes bravely about her work, resolute, silent, uncomplaining. The children grow up pretty much as fate dictates. Even when very small they seem well able to protect themselves. The wife of one of my teamsters, who lived in a small outlying camp, used to keep the youngest and most troublesome members of her family out of mischief by the simple expedient of picketing them out, each child being tied by the leg, with a long leather string, to a stake driven into the ground, so that it could neither get at another child nor at anything breakable.

The best buckskin maker that I ever met was, if not a typical frontiers-woman, at least a woman who could not have reached her full development save on the border. She made first-class hunting-shirts, leggins, and gantlets. When I knew her she was living alone in her cabin on mid-prairie, having dismissed her husband six months previously in an exceedingly summary manner. She not only possessed redoubtable qualities of head and hand, but also a nice sense of justice, even towards Indians, that is not always found on the frontier. Once, going there for a buckskin shirt, I met at her cabin three Sioux, and from their leader, named One Bull, purchased a tobacco pouch, beautifully worked with porcupine quills. She had given them some dinner, for which they had paid with a deer-hide. Falling into conversation, she mentioned that just before I came up a white man, apparently from Deadwood, had passed by, and had tried to steal the Indians' horses. The latter had been too quick for him, had run him down, and brought him back to the cabin. "I told 'em to go right on and hang him, and *I* wouldn't never cheep about it," said my informant; "but they let him go, after taking his gun. There ain't no sense in stealing from Indians any more than from white folks, and I'm not going to have it round my ranch, neither. There! I'll give 'em back the deer-hide they give me for the dinner and things, anyway." I told her that I sincerely wished we could make her sheriff and Indian agent. She made the Indians — and whites, too, for that matter — behave themselves and walk the straightest kind of line, not tolerating the least symptom of rebellion, but she had a strong natural sense of justice.

The cowboy balls spoken of above are always great events in the small towns where they take place. Being usually given when the round-up passes near, everybody round about comes in for them. They are almost always conducted with great decorum; no unseemly conduct would be tolerated. There is usually some master of the ceremonies, chosen with due regard to brawn as well as brain. He calls off the figures of the square dances so that even the inexperienced may get through them, and incidentally preserves order. Sometimes we are allowed to wear our revolvers, and sometimes not. The nature of the band, of course, depends upon the size of the place. I remember one ball that came near being a failure because our half-breed fiddler "went and got himself shot," as the indignant master of the ceremonies phrased it.

But all these things are merely incidents in the cowboy's life. It is utterly unfair to judge the whole class by what a few individuals do in the course of two or three days spent in town, instead of by the long months of weary, honest toil common to all alike. To appreciate properly his fine, manly qualities, the wild rough-rider of the plains should be seen in his own home. There he passes his days; there he does his life-work; there, when he meets death, he faces it as he has faced many other evils, with quiet, uncomplaining fortitude. Brave, hospitable, hardy, and adventurous, he is the grim pioneer of our race; he prepares the way for the civilization from before whose face he must himself disappear. Hard and dangerous though his existence is, it has yet a wild attraction that strongly draws to it his bold, free spirit. He lives in the lonely lands where mighty rivers twist in long reaches between the barren bluffs; where the prairies stretch out into billowy plains of waving grass, girt only by the blue horizon — plains across whose endless breadth he can steer his course for days and weeks and see neither man to speak to nor hill to break the level; where the glory and the burning splendor of the sunsets kindle the blue vault of heaven and the level brown earth till they merge together in an ocean of flaming fire.

Theodore Roosevelt.

89